SOVIET FOREIGN POLICY, THE LEAGUE OF NATIONS AND EUROPE, 1917–1939

SOVIET FOREIGN POLICY, THE LEAGUE OF NATIONS AND EUROPE, 1917–1939

R. H. Haigh
D. S. Morris
A. R. Peters

BARNES & NOBLE BOOKS
TOTOWA, NEW JERSEY

First published in the USA in 1986 by

Barnes & Noble Books,
81 Adams Drive,
Totowa, New Jersey
07512

ISBN: 0-389-20611-3

Printed in Great Britain by Blackmore Press, Shaftesbury, Dorset

Contents

Acknowledgements

A number of people deserve our thanks for the support and encouragement which they have given us during the writing of this work. For financial assistance we are indebted to the D. Thacker Special Research Fund of Sheffield City Polytechnic and to the Nuffield Foundation. Mrs Margot Nadin and her team at the Inter-Library Loan Service of the Eric Mensforth Library gave cheerfully of their time and effort to secure source material. Mrs Ruth Barker has typed the manuscript from drafts which left much to be desired in terms of legibility. Bob Haigh and Dave Morris owe particular thanks to the Department of Politics at the University of Leicester and the School of Peace Studies at the University of Bradford, respectively, for the all too short time they spent there as Visiting Research Fellows and for the warmth of reception they were accorded; in particular they would like to acknowledge the special debts they owe to Professor Jack Spence and Dr Nigel Young. Finally, our families deserve not only to be mentioned but to be thanked most sincerely for their tolerance and understanding of our neglect of them during the three years in which this work was in preparation; to them our efforts are dedicated.

R. H. Haigh
D. S. Morris
A. R. Peters
Sheffield, 1985

Preface

This book represents but part of a wider study of the origins of the Molotov–Ribbentrop Pact (Nazi–Soviet Non-Aggression Pact) of 1939. When considering the course of European interwar diplomacy extensive attention has been devoted to the analysis of the relationships established between Britain, France, Italy and Germany. Within this framework numerous historians have attempted to analyse the various crises of the interwar era and to account for the events which eventually propelled Europe into a second world war. Yet it is difficult to discount the role played by the Soviet Union in the network of intrigue and manoeuvre that was a feature of interwar diplomacy. The Soviet Union cannot glibly be dismissed as the outcast of Europe. Although initially the Soviet regime set a defiant face to the outside world, within five years of its inception the attendance of a Soviet delegation at the Genoa Conference and the conclusion of the Treaty of Rapallo signalled the acceptance by the Soviet leadership of the need to establish formal channels of communication with the outside world. If the establishment of diplomatic links could be justified as a means of preventing the creation of an anti-Soviet European cartel there was also a recognition of the need to enlist the industrial expertise of the industrialised western world as the Soviet Union prepared itself for a lengthy period of 'coexistence' with its capitalist neighbours.

Although the era of 'peaceful coexistence' was initially launched by Lenin it was Stalin who propelled the Soviet Union once again into the mainstream of international diplomacy. In many respects the relationship established in this period between the Soviet Union and the

League of Nations reflected the evolution of Soviet foreign policy as it attempted to adjust to the problems posed to Soviet territorial integrity in the interwar period. As the child of Versailles, Lenin initially regarded the League as the instrument of rampant capitalism yet within two decades the Soviet Union accepted the principles of the Covenant and full membership of the League. By an ironic twist of fate Soviet delegates to Geneva in the latter half of the 1930s found themselves allied with their British and French counterparts in attempting to defend the European *status quo*.

Just how the wheel turned full circle from 'revolutionary war' to the defence of 'collective security' is examined using the following format:

1. 1919–33: The move from 'revolutionary war' to 'peaceful co-existence'.
2. 1933–35: The period of readjustment. Soviet membership of the League of Nations and the promotion of the United Front.
3. 1935–38: Collective security put to the test — Abyssinia, the Rhineland, Austria and Czechoslovakia.
4. The collapse of collective security and the signing of the Molotov–Ribbentrop Pact.

It is contended that throughout this period Soviet foreign policy was dictated by the requirements of an aggressive ideology tempered by 'realpolitik'. In this context, despite the opening of diplomatic links and professions of sincerity, Soviet relations with the European powers were continually shrouded with thinly-veiled mistrust and suspicion. Yet, through the agency of the League of Nations and the opening of channels of communication with the major actors in the European theatre, the Soviet Union played arguably an influential role in the diplomat intrigue of the 1930s and probably a decisive part in the events which led to war in September 1939.

1 Defending the Revolution

The success of the Bolshevik revolution in November 1917 not only shook the foundations of Russian society but also sent tremors throughout Europe.[1] The determination to transform the European war into a revolutionary war was proclaimed by the Soviet Commissar for Foreign Affairs, Trotsky, on 19 December 1917:

> We do not attempt to conceal the fact that we do not consider the existing capitalist Governments capable of making a democratic peace. The revolutionary struggle of the toiling masses against the existing Governments can alone bring Europe nearer to such a peace. Its full realization can only be guaranteed by the victorious proletarian revolution in all capitalist countries.[2]

Trotsky was convinced that the events of November 1917 could not be viewed in isolation, but rather represented the first phase of a global uprising by the oppressed against their capitalist overlords. There could, therefore, be no compromise with the capitalist nations whose interests were diametrically opposed to the Bolshevik revolution.[3] The belief that a period of confrontation and conflict with the capitalist powers was inevitable was reaffirmed by Lenin in a declaration to the Eighth Party Congress of the Russian Communist Party:

> it is inconceivable that the Soviet republic should continue to exist for a long period side by side with imperialist states. Ultimately one or the other must conquer. Until this end occurs a number of terrible clashes between the Soviet republic and bourgeois states is inevitable.[4]

From the outset, therefore, Soviet foreign policy assumed a hostile and aggressive stance to the outside world. Through the agency of the Third International (Comintern), formed in March 1919, the Bolshevik leadership sought to foment social revolution on a global scale.[5] Yet, in most instances, the resources at the disposal of the Soviet regime were pitifully inadequate. Theodore von Laue subsequently noted of the problems confronting Lenin and Trotsky:

> With the resources of imperial Russia which had been so recently found wanting and which were further reduced by loss of territory and civil war, the Bolsheviks tried to sustain a political ambition far exceeding the boldest aspirations of the Tsars. The discrepancy between a weakness so recently demonstrated and an ambition so boldly proclaimed would have forever discredited the Soviet leaders, had they not developed, at ferocious cost, two novel sources of power: a totalitarian dictatorship to expand Russia's military and industrial potential; and a totalitarian type of foreign relations.[6]

There seemed, however, to be no alternative, for unless European revolution destroyed the military might of the major powers, they would almost certainly unite to crush the Soviet state at birth.[7] Only by adopting an aggressive stance and by mobilising the military and propaganda resources at its disposal could the Soviet Union hope to survive.[8]

Initially, this policy of confrontation appeared to be justified. The belief in the imminence of revolution was fuelled by uprisings in Germany, Hungary and Poland during 1919 and 1920. Yet, with the advance of the White armies the pressure on the Soviet state increased almost daily. In an attempt to prevent the collapse of the Bolshevik revolution Lenin was forced to seek a temporary understanding with the capitalist powers.[9] The possibility of a temporary détente had been suggested by the conclusion of the Treaty of Brest-Litovsk in March 1918 which, at a heavy territorial price, had effectively halted the march of the central powers into the Soviet heartland.[10] In a speech to the Central Executive Committee on 14 May 1918, Lenin indicated that further agreements with the western powers might have to be engineered:

> We must stick to our waiting tactics and exploit the conflicts and antagonisms among the imperialists, slowly accumulating strength and maintaining the oasis of Soviet power in the middle of the raging imperialist sea.[11]

With reference to the possibility of an attack by the capitalist powers Lenin continued:

> We shall do the little we can whatever diplomacy is capable of doing, to put off that moment; we shall do everything to prolong that brief and precarious respite which we got in March.[12]

This decision, however, was underwritten by the conviction that diplomacy could only delay but not halt the determination of the western powers to destroy the Bolshevik state before revolutionary fervour took root throughout Europe.

In this light, in the post-war period the newly-created League of Nations was seen as a symbol of capitalist hostility. Orchestrated by Britain and France, which had played a leading role in excluding the Soviet Union from the Paris Peace Conference, the League seemed to represent a coalition of capitalist interests seeking to destroy the Soviet state.[13] Furthermore, given the material and financial assistance provided by Britain and France to the White generals in their struggle against the Red Army, it appeared that steps were already being taken actively to overthrow the Bolshevik regime.[14] It was hardly surprising, therefore, that the First Congress of the Communist International denounced the League as 'the Holy Alliance of the bourgeoisie for the suppression of the proletarian revolution'.[15] Bolshevik fears were certainly not unfounded as Fritz Epstein noted:

> It cannot be doubted that in Paris the League of Nations had been regarded at its beginning as an instrument which could be used for defence against, or even to crush, the Bolshevist influence.[16]

Although few went as far as Winston Churchill in proposing that the League of Nations organise 'collective intervention by a composed force'[17] to overthrow the Bolshevik government, both Clemençeau and Lloyd-George were prepared to consider schemes whereby the Baltic states, the Ukraine and the Caucasus would be detached from the Russian nation and assume the status of mandated states under the supervision of the League of Nations.[18] It was apparent that the members of the League had little or no sympathy for the Soviet state and therefore, in response, it was hardly surprising that the Bolsheviks consistently denied the legitimacy of the League of Nations as a regulatory agency in the conduct of international affairs. In a letter to President Wilson, dated 21 October 1918, Chicherin, the Soviet Commissar for Foreign Affairs, pointed out that the Soviet Union could not accept the definition of national self-determination applied by the League of Nations to the Russian borderlands when at the same time its implications for the status of Ireland, Egypt and India were apparently denied.[19] Furthermore, he continued, the Soviet Union could not accept the impartial adjudication of the League of Nations in the redrawing of national boundaries when the League was so patently dominated by nations antagonistic to the interests of the Bolshevik state. In a note to the British government on 17 July 1920 Chicherin expanded this theme:

> The Soviet Government can in no way agree that one group of Powers should assume the role of supreme body over all the states in the world. Watching over the full inviolability of the sovereign rights of the Russian working people, the Soviet Government absolutely rejects the pretensions of any foreign groups of Powers claiming to assume the role of supreme masters of the fate of other nations.[20]

The possibility, however, of mandates being established over vast tracts of the former Tsarist state tentatively assumed that the country had been effectively divided into autonomous units. The successful campaign undertaken by the Red Army in the period 1919–20 against the various secessionist and anti-Bolshevik elements to all intents and purposes rendered further deliberation of the mandate issue, short of direct military intervention, largely irrelevant.[21]

Although the internal authority of the Bolshevik party within the Soviet Union had been effectively stabilised by the end of 1920, the party hierarchy appreciated that, with the failure of the communist uprisings in Germany and Hungary, and the defeat of the Red Army at the gates of Warsaw, there seemed very little prospect of revolution within Europe in the immediate future.[22] While reasserting his belief in the inevitability of the overthrow of capitalism, Lenin conceded that there would have to be a 'breathing space' while the conditions for revolution ripened. As a result, while not detracting from the continued work of the Communist International in fostering the conditions for revolution, the accent of Soviet foreign policy began to move towards a more defensive posture. Frederick Schumann later noted:

> The victory of World Revolution might have meant global peace had it eventuated in a worldwide union of proletarian dictatorships in which national sovereignty and international anarchy would both have disappeared. The defeat of World Revolution necessarily obliged Moscow to defend the sovereignty of the Soviet State in an anarchic world of sovereignties in which all others were 'bourgeois' and therefore actually or potentially anti-Soviet.[23]

Lenin appreciated that if long-term Soviet interests were best served by a détente with the capitalist world, then this was the path along which he would have to lead the Soviet people despite the protests of the left-wing revolutionaries led by Zinoviev and Trotsky.[24]

The first confirmation of this reassessment of Bolshevik strategy was provided by the presence of a Soviet delegation at the Genoa conference in April 1922.[25] The mere presence of the delegation was indicative of the Soviet desire to open a dialogue with the western powers. From the outset of the conference it was apparent that the Soviet delegation acknowledged the need to enlist foreign economic aid to rebuild the war-shattered Soviet economy.[26] At the first plenary session Chicherin pointed to the need to promote international economic collaboration:

> Whilst maintaining the standpoint of their communist principles, the Russian delegation recognise that in the present period of history, which permits the parallel existence of the old social order and of the new order now being born, economic collaboration between the states representing these two systems of property is imperatively necessary for the general economic reconstruction.[27]

Indeed, the acquisition of trade links with the European states was imperative for the success of the New Economic Policy launched in the spring of 1921.[28] Yet despite the conclusion of trade agreements with Britain and Germany suspicion of the western powers was still evident in Soviet calculations.[29] Chicherin therefore suspected that the conference would be used to mobilise a European economic cartel capable of holding the Soviet Union to ransom.[30] In order to forestall such a development, the Soviet delegation opened clandestine negotiations with Weimar Germany.[31] The outcome was the Treaty of Rapallo of which Kennan subsequently noted:

> It was not a treaty of alliance. It had no secret clauses or protocols. It consisted basically, only of provisions for the establishment of full diplomatic relations, for the mutual renunciation of claims (which relieved the Germans of the nightmare of Article 116, and meant, for the Russians, conversely that there would be at least *one* great power which could not advance claims for the losses of its nationals in Russia), and for the extension of most-favoured-nation treatment in commercial matters and in the treatment of nationals.[32]

While outwardly a rather innocuous agreement, Rapallo in fact represented a major breakthrough for Soviet diplomacy. Not only did the treaty incorporate official diplomatic recognition of the Soviet state, but in addition it established the basis for a relationship with Berlin that would give the Soviet nation access to European industrial and technical expertise. The need to establish such links had been outlined at the Ninth Congress of the Communist Party in March 1921:

> The opportunity thus provided for new relations between the Soviet Republic and capitalist countries, based on treaties and

> agreements, should be used in the first place to raise the productive powers of the Republic to improve the position of the primary productive force — the working class.[33]

Of even greater satisfaction to Chicherin, however, was the belief that Rapallo represented the detachment of Germany from the clutches of Britain and France and, therefore, the possibility of the Soviet Union being confronted by a united and hostile European bloc had been reduced.

Previous Soviet overtures in the field of diplomacy had centred on the establishment of treaties of friendship with Persia, Turkey and Afghanistan.[34] The purpose of this strategy was to neutralise the border states in an attempt to prevent their use as bases for foreign military intervention. In addition, the opening of diplomatic relations also provided a propaganda platform for the Comintern in its campaign to promote revolution against the colonial powers in Asia. The Treaty of Rapallo, however, represented a significant advance on this strategy.[35] Theodore von Laue noted of Rapallo: 'The tie not only weakened the force of capitalist encirclement but, through the influx of German experts, directly assisted the socialist reconstruction of Russia.'[36] In the quest for survival the Soviet regime was moving into an era of tacit détente with the capitalist world. It was a period that was characterised by the assertion of the possibility of 'peaceful coexistence' and, following the failure of the communist uprising in Germany in 1923, the relative subjugation of revolutionary incitement in favour of the establishment of normal diplomatic relations with the outside world.[37] The Soviet desire to open extensive relations with the international community was indicated by Chicherin's report to the Central Executive Committee on 18 October 1924:

> Our government has more than once declared that it considers possible a participation in periodic congresses of all countries of the world on a basis of full equality.[38]

Indeed, as early as 1921, informal contacts had been created between the Soviet Union and the League of Nations. These links were reinforced the following year when a Soviet delegation attended a conference organised by the League of Nations Health Organisation in Warsaw to establish measures to combat epidemics.[39] If, however, it was hoped that the Soviet Union would be offered full membership of the League, such illusions were rudely shattered by the reaction in London and Paris to the conclusion of the Treaty of Rapallo.[40] The treaty was seen as an attempt to detach Germany from the western camp and, therefore, as a thinly-veiled assault on the status quo established in Europe by the Versailles settlement.[41] The treaty, therefore, fuelled western hostility to the Soviet Union and relations deteriorated further in the summer of 1923 following the assassination of the Soviet envoy, Vorovsky, at Lausanne.[42] The Soviet decision to boycott further meetings on Swiss territory only served to further hinder relations between Moscow and the major European powers.[43]

In the following year the Soviet Union once again returned to the offensive and publicly vilified the role of the League. In October Chicherin declared that the League was

> a poorly-screened coalition of victor-Powers created in order to secure their acquisitions and conquests.[44]

> Entry into the present League of Nations means, in the opinion of our Government, the surrender of its independent policy and subjection to the policy of the Entente powers.[45]

In addition, the Soviet *Encyclopedia of State and Law* (1925–26) defined the League of Nations as: 'a political combination or a group of nations interested in the preservation and utilisation of the post war international status quo'.[46] Relations between the League and the Soviet Union were further exacerbated by the suggestion that the League adopt the role of arbitrator in determining the sovereignty of the Åaland Islands and the reconciliation of disputes surrounding the establishment of definitive frontiers between Poland and Lithuania and Poland and the Soviet Union. Chicherin immediately denounced this proposal as a further attempt by the western powers to meddle in Soviet affairs.[47]

It appeared, therefore, that the gap between Geneva and Moscow in this period was unbridgeable. While the Soviet Union continued to maintain informal links with the League of Nations Health Organisation and despatched observers to several League meetings, there was no suggestion that moves were afoot to remove the barriers to full Soviet membership.[48] Indeed, in all probability the Soviet government was not entirely displeased with this situation.[49] Although out to disrupt an anti-Soviet western alliance and also to enlist western economic aid, the attainment of full League status was not a priority for the Soviet leadership. The conclusion of non-aggression pacts in 1925 and 1926 with Lithuania, Turkey, Persia and Afghanistan indicated that Moscow was largely preoccupied with securing its frontiers from assault. In this context to have accepted the wide-ranging commitment envisaged by the Covenant of the League of Nations to maintain collective security would not have been compatible with Soviet strategy in this period.[50]

The suspicion and hostility which still pervaded relations between Geneva and Moscow were indicated by the reaction of the Soviet leadership in 1926 to the announcement that Germany was to be invited to join the League of Nations.[51] This decision was seen as a bid to create an extensive anti-Soviet bloc of states within the League of Nations, with the eventual intention of promoting an anti-Bolshevik crusade under the guise of applying sanctions under Article 16 of the Covenant against the Soviet Union.[52] Soviet fears were only subsequently mollified when, with the conclusion of the Treaty of Berlin on 26 April 1926, the German government confirmed that it would not be a party to any form of aggression against the Soviet Union.[53]

Although the acknowledgement of the need for a period of retrenchment while the conditions necessary for world revolution developed was initially directed by Lenin, the conviction that this breathing space could mature into a period of lengthy coexistence with the capitalist world is generally associated with the influence of Stalin.[54] Stalin was highly sceptical as to the imminence of world revolution and as early as June 1925 predicted that the Soviet Union would remain the sole bastion of communism for at least 20 years.[55] In this context Stalin identified the task ahead as one of developing the internal strength and physical security of the Soviet state. Von Laue later noted:

> The old policy seemed no longer adequate; the direct incitement of revolution became increasingly ineffectual and even ridiculous. Zinoviev's miserable Reval *putsch* in December 1924 was the last expression of this policy.[56]
>
> A group called the 'economists' eager to rebuild Russian prosperity even with foreign assistance advocated less revolution and more foreign trade which could be obtained only with the help of diplomacy.[57]

The product of this strategy was the first Five Year Plan, launched in 1928 with the aim of completely rebuilding Soviet heavy industry. Within this framework the revolutionary role was further devalued in favour of further 'normalisation' of relations with the major European powers while the programme of economic reconstruction was launched.[58] Ian Grey observed of this period:

> at no time was peace more crucially necessary than during this first plan when the whole nation was extended and concentrated on the gigantic tasks of collectivisation and industrialisation. War at this time would have meant the collapse of the economy and of the nation. The demand for peace, reiterated by all members of the Soviet government, was undoubtedly sincere.[59]

The natural consequence of this decision was a diminution of the activities of the Comintern:

> From the 'vanguards of world revolution' the Communist parties became in Trotsky's words, the more or less pacifist 'frontier guards' of Soviet Russia. From Stalin's viewpoint it would have been utter folly to risk the substance of socialism in one country for the shadow of revolution abroad.[60]

The corollary of this strategy was the expansion of the role of the Ministry of Foreign Affairs (Narkomindel)[61] as the Soviet Union strove to present an acceptable face to the major powers. Von Laue argued that the Soviet Union in this period 'took a line which might be called homeopathic revolution; it would be progressive, anti-capitalist, even proletarian, but without the Bolshevik sting.'[62] However, there was little immediate indication of a revision of strategy. In December 1927 Stalin declared:

> Two years ago one could talk about a period of relative balance between the Soviets and the capitalist countries and about their 'peaceful coexistence'. Now we have every reason to say that the period of 'peaceful coexistence' recedes into the past, giving place to a period of imperialist attacks and of preparation of intervention against the USSR.[63]

This conviction appeared to be prompted by the decision, during the course of 1927, by both Britain and China to cut their diplomatic relations with the Soviet Union and revert to stances of outward hostility.[64] With regard to the League of Nations, Stalin stated:

> the League of Nations is an organisation designed to make preparations for war . . .
>
> if we were to enter the League of Nations we should only have the choice between hammer and anvil. Now, we neither wish to be a hammer for the weak nations nor yet an anvil for the strong ones.[65]

In addition, in April 1927, the Soviet Prime Minister, Rykov, poured scorn on the idea of a world disarmament conference to be convened under the aegis of the League of Nations:

> The League of Nations is endeavouring to prove its pacifism by convening a disarmament conference. But the preparatory work of the conference indicates that it is less a disarmament conference than a conference to discuss how to maintain, with the least expenditure, the military rule of those countries which at present still dominate the whole world.[66]

Yet, while outwardly bellicose, it was apparent that Stalin was increasingly preoccupied with the problem of carrying through a massive reconstruction of the Soviet economy. If the Soviet Union wished to regain the status of a great power, it had to harness its internal resources to better effect.[67] Economic development, however, could not be achieved without a period of international stability and security. In this light Stalin's prediction of the possibility of a resumption of imperialist intervention was probably designed for internal consumption.[68] The need to mobilise the resources of the Soviet Union to respond to a perceived external threat was to be used as the justification for the vast reorganisation of the Soviet industrial and agricultural bases to be undertaken over the following decade.

It would seem, therefore, that in the sphere of international relations, the defensive ethos of Soviet policy was maintained. The need to establish détente with the major European powers was indicated by the positive steps taken by the Soviet Union in 1927 towards active participation in the affairs of the international community. In May 1927, following a guarantee from the Swiss government concerning the safety of Soviet citizens on Swiss territory, a Soviet delegation attended an international economic conference held at Geneva.[69] Furthermore, despite previous denunciations of the League of Nations, the Soviet Union accepted an invitation to attend the Fourth Session of the Preparatory Commission on Disarmament held at Geneva in November 1927 under the auspices of the League of Nations.[70] The Soviet delegate, Maxim Litvinov, justified this decision by declaring:

> To us the representatives of the Soviet Union and exponents of definite socio-economic theories, the impossibility of removing the politico-economic antagonisms of capitalist society, and hence the ultimate inevitability of war is perfectly clear. We believe, however, or we should not be here, that the danger of war might be considerably diminished, or made comparatively remote, by some measure of real disarmament.[71]

Litvinov referred to the Moscow Conference of December 1922 as evidence of the Soviet dedication to the cause of disarmament and, in his initial speech at Geneva, proposed that the Commission adopt the principle of complete abolition of all air, marine and land forces.[72] This initiative was followed, in March 1928, with the presentation of a Draft Convention on Disarmament which challenged the League to accept the principle of total disarmament:

> 1. Does the Commission agree to base its further labour on the principle of complete and general disarmament during the periods proposed by us
>
> and,
>
> 2. Is it prepared to carry out the first stage of disarmament so as

> to make the conduct of war, if not an absolute impossibility, of extreme difficulty in a year's time?[73]

Only Turkey and Germany supported the Soviet proposals.[74] In rejecting Litvinov's contention that peace was indivisible, the French delegation maintained that disarmament would have to be linked to some form of security agreement if the fear of aggression was to be effectively eliminated during the period of disarmament. Indeed, throughout the conference it would appear that the major powers regarded Litvinov's pleas for international collaboration with the utmost suspicion.[75] It was difficult to reconcile Litvinov's pronouncements with the efforts of the Comintern to foment revolution in Western Europe. As Max Beloff later noted:

> As a weak power in the military sense, the Soviet Union had everything to gain from disarmament proposals, however radical. At the same time, the USSR could usefully and safely proclaim its adherence to the doctrine of disarmament, even when there was no hope of achieving anything, in order to embarrass the capitalist states by showing up the hypocrisy of their 'pacifism'.[76]

All in all, the French and British had every reason to suspect that Litvinov was seeking to use the international platform of Geneva to further Soviet interests by embarrassing the western powers for their failure to find a formula for disarmament.[77] Furthermore the Soviet advocation of total disarmament was seen as a ploy to widen the ground between Germany, on the one hand, and France and Britain on the other.[78]

Yet to maintain that the Soviet Union was motivated purely by self-interest is probably unjust. The choice of Maxim Litvinov as Soviet delegate to the Preparatory Commission on Disarmament rather than Chicherin, Commissar for Foreign Affairs, was in itself significant. Chicherin was innately hostile to the League of Nations.[79] Louis Fischer claimed that in a conversation with him, in 1930, Chicherin stated: 'I am and always have been an absolutely undiluted, unmixed, unwavering, unswerving enemy of our joining the League of Nations.'[80] Litvinov, however, was identified with the growing school of thought that believed in the possibility of a working relationship between the Soviet Union and the capitalist world. Henry L. Roberts concluded:

> to him perhaps more than to any other single person may be traced the impression that revolutionary Russia was returning to the family of nations and could be counted upon as a force for stability and peace.[81]

The emergence of Litvinov as Soviet spokesman in Geneva was

apparently indicative of a growing resolve to establish a *rapprochement* with the major powers. The eventual decision by the Soviet Union to dissociate itself from the draft treaty produced by the Preparatory Commission in November 1930 was, therefore, a disappointment but did not deflect Litvinov from his ultimate goal.[82] The failure to reach agreement can be credited to the difficulties of achieving a compromise when the major powers were themselves divided in terms of reconciling disarmament with the problem of what could be considered adequate guarantees of security. The nature of the draft treaty revealed that this problem was never firmly resolved. In addition, the determination of Britain, France, Italy, Japan and the United States to settle most of the major points of contention in private discussions only served further to undermine confidence in the purpose of the proceedings at Geneva.[83] On leaving Geneva, following the final session of the Preparatory Commission on Disarmament, Litvinov stated:

> certain Powers which, thanks to the quantitative and qualitative superiority of their armaments, occupy a dominating position in the world arena and are anxious to maintain and extend their domination, have firmly decided on no account to reduce their military strength. Instead of helping to expose these trends before public opinion, the preparatory commission concealed them, and, taking the line of least resistance, and anxious for apparent unanimity, fell into line with precisely those delegations which represented the tendency not to permit disarmament to which I have referred.[84]

The only firm international commitment entered into by the Soviet Union in this period was its adherence to the Kellogg–Briand Pact in August 1928. Attitudes amongst the Soviet hierarchy to the pact, which renounced recourse to war for the solution of disputes, were mixed. The Soviet Prime Minister, Rykov, dismissed the pact in the following terms in May 1929: 'The Kellogg pact cannot be regarded as a factor in the prevention of war, as this document contains no real guarantees against war.'[85] Litvinov, however, perceived that certain benefits could be derived from the agreement. Certainly, by embracing the principle of non-aggression it would be difficult for the western powers to justify the assertion that the Soviet state was a threat to world security. In addition, Litvinov was able to use the terms of the pact as a basis for a series of non-aggression treaties with Poland, Lithuania, Turkey, Persia, Danzig, Rumania, Latvia and Estonia during 1929. With the exception of Finland, the Litvinov Protocol effectively neutralised the states bordering the Soviet Union as possible bases for foreign intervention against the Soviet Union.[86]

The Litvinov Protocol underlined the fact that domestic security remained the paramount consideration in Soviet strategy. On assuming the position of Commissar for Foreign Affairs in July 1930, Litvinov outlined his thoughts on the future course of Soviet foreign policy:

> We have to build socialism in our country surrounded by capitalist countries occupying five-sixths of the earth's surface. We cannot ignore it, and we are therefore trying to discover and to put into operation methods for the peaceful coexistence of the two social systems. We have, and still have in the future, to make the greatest efforts to combat the aggressive tendencies of certain capitalist groupings making for the creation of constant dispute, and conflicts between the two systems; therefore these efforts will be directed to the consolidation and maintenance of peace among the Nations.[87]

Schuman, however, subsequently questioned the nature of this apparent dedication to the cause of international stability:

> Neutrality is the antithesis of collective security. The Soviet peace pacts of the 1920s were in principle and purpose the negation of the League Covenant. The latter sought to generalize war by obligating all States to join forces against aggressors. The former sought to localize war by obligating each signatory to remain aloof from any conflict in which the other might be involved. For Moscow, as for Washington, the formula for peace was not the Wilsonian precept of 'making any war everybody's business' but rather the injunction of 'keeping out of other people's wars'.[88]

The absence of any real understanding between the Soviet Union and the western powers was illustrated by the Soviet reaction to Briand's launching of a scheme, under the aegis of the League of Nations, to promote federal bonds within Europe on both an economic and political level.[89] Litvinov suspected that it was little more than an attempt to unite Europe economically against the Soviet Union. In July 1930 he claimed:

> we encounter inimical tendencies among certain hostile capitalist groupings, who are conducting a campaign for the severance of economic relations with our Union. Their efforts appear to be directed chiefly against our exports, but in fact they are against our entire foreign trade.[90]

His decision, therefore, to accept an invitation to attend the third session of the Commission of Enquiry into the Briand Plan was motivated essentially by a determination to prevent the creation of a

European cartel dedicated to controlling trade with the Soviet Union. *Pravda* brazenly declared:

> By taking part in the work of the European Commission, the Soviet Union will wreck the plans of the leaders of the Commission, plans for the secret elaboration of anti-Soviet projects.[91]

It was rather fanciful, however, to believe that the Briand Plan was primarily anti-Soviet or that Litvinov was capable of scuttling the scheme. In fact, the proposals finally floundered when they were less than wholeheartedly embraced by the British government.[92] It has to be noted, however, that the presence of Soviet delegations at international gatherings was becoming increasingly commonplace in this period. The Soviet representatives, however, adopted a rather enigmatic approach. While anxious to gain the benefits that might derive from collaboration with the western nations, the Soviet Union avoided positive commitments and rarely refused the opportunity to embarrass the western powers over their failure to promote post-war economic and political cooperation. It was not surprising, therefore, that the western powers viewed Litvinov's performances at Geneva with a certain amount of scepticism. The suspicion that he sought to drive a wedge between them by exploiting their differences was reaffirmed by his pronouncements at the Disarmament Conference convened in Geneva in February 1932. From the outset it was evident that a consensus on the format of disarmament did not exist. In reply to the French proposal that an international military force be created to perform a policing role under the direction of the League of Nations, Litvinov reverted to the stance originally adopted in 1927: 'Security against war must be created. This security can never be achieved by roundabout ways, but only by the direct way of total general disarmament.'[93]

The inherent suspicion of a force that could possibly be manipulated by the western powers to topple the Soviet regime was sufficient to create total Soviet opposition to the Tardieu scheme. In its opposition to the French scheme the Soviet Union found an ally in Germany. The German government suspected that the Tardieu Plan was being utilised to defend French interests and prevent any discussion of German demands for equality of armaments.[94] F. P. Walters concluded of the initial negotiations:

> The general feeling therefore was that France had put forward her plan not with any hope that it might be carried out, but as a justification of her determination to retain her own armaments and make no concessions to Germany.[95]

In an attempt to break this deadlock both Britain and the United

States of America introduced schemes based on qualitative disarmament to a level acceptable to both France and Germany.[96] While Litvinov, who in 1928 had pointed to the need to distinguish between offensive and defensive weaponry, welcomed the move, it was apparent, by July 1932, that the powers were deadlocked in their attempt to define offensive and defensive weapons.[97] In such circumstances the conference threatened to dissolve into piecemeal horse-trading amongst the major powers:

> It was once more, said Litvinov, the postponement of all real decisions and the renewal of these private discussions to which recourse had been so often and always without result. 'I vote for disarmament' he concluded 'but against the resolution.'[98]

The second year of the Disarmament Conference opened with a solution to the problems apparently no nearer. Indeed, Germany's withdrawal from the conference for a period of four months was indicative of the increasing difficulties being encountered.[99] As F. P. Walters noted, this stalemate was ultimately to work to the advantage of the revisionist powers:

> those Allied leaders . . . who spoke as though Germany could be kept disarmed by a mere refusal to discuss the bases of a settlement by consent were deluding themselves and criminally misleading their fellow countrymen.[100]

Yet while Britain, France, Germany and the United States wrangled over the format of disarmament and security measures, the Soviet Union remained primarily concerned with further insulating its defensive posture. In this respect Litvinov contributed actively to the debate on the definition of aggression for it presented a further opportunity to gain recognition that military or economic action against the Soviet Union would represent an infringement of international law.[101] Furthermore, Litvinov used a definition of aggression accepted at the conference as the basis for a multilateral non-aggression treaty concluded in July 1933 with eleven neighbouring states.[102] Henry L. Roberts noted of this extension of the Litvinov Protocol:

> Thus the Soviet Union was at this time definitely less interested in establishing a criterion for aggression which could provide the basis for collective measures — than in protecting its position as a revolutionary state in a presumably hostile world.[103]

Litvinov appeared, therefore, to be primarily concerned with international recognition of the Soviet state.[104] Yet in the spring of 1933 the Soviet Commissar began to adopt a more flexible stance. In response to the MacDonald Plan, which in March 1933 presented the conference with a comprehensive set of proposals for disarmament and future security. Litvinov indicated that the Soviet Union was now interested in exploring an open-ended security arrangement.[105] This departure from his previous preoccupation with regional security measures was indicative of the emergence of new perspectives in Soviet foreign policy deliberations.[106] The decision by Germany, in 1933, to leave the League of Nations and the Japanese refusal to accept any form of armament limitation apparently confirmed the growing conviction that the stability of the post-war international system was being subjected to increasing strain.[107] In this context 1933 was a significant year for Soviet foreign policy for the principles that had guided the format of policy for almost a decade had to be carefully re-examined.

The first indication of a shift in Soviet strategy was provided by the decision, in May, to sell the Soviet interest in the Chinese Eastern Railway to the Japanese puppet-state of Manchukuo.[108] This attempt to defuse possible sources of Soviet–Japanese tension was precipitated by an appreciation of the changing balance of powers in the Far East.[109] As Ian Grey subsequently noted:

> the balance of power in the Far East had changed drastically. Russia had been greatly weakened; China had been paralysed by the collapse of the old dynasty and by revolution; Germany had been eliminated; the Western powers were distracted by other problems. Japan occupied a particularly strong position and was ready to grasp at this opportunity to extend her possessions on the mainland.[110]

The threat presented by resurgent Japanese militarism to Soviet territory in the Far East and, in particular, to the Soviet sponsored Republic of Outer Mongolia was implicit. While an eventual clash of interests between the Soviet Union and Japan seemed inevitable, the immediate task was to postpone the confrontation until it could be conducted on terms favourable to the Soviet Union.[111] Following the rejection by Japan of Soviet overtures for a pact of non-aggression, Litvinov reverted to a policy of appeasement. In attempting to account for the Soviet Union's refusal to condemn the Japanese invasion of Manchuria,[112] Litvinov later admitted:

> We declined to take part in the international actions undertaken and planned at that time, first, because we did not believe in the honesty and consistency of the governments participating in these actions and primarily because we did not seek, nor do we now seek, armed conflict with Japan.[113]

More particularly, Soviet suspicion of the League was fuelled by the conviction that the European powers, rather than seeking to restrain Japan,[114] would welcome the opening of hostilities between Japan and the Soviet Union.[115]

The Soviet Union, therefore, refused to accept the report of the Lytton Commission set up by the League of Nations to investigate the Manchurian conflict and also declined an invitation to participate on an Advisory Committee established in February 1933 to implement the recommendations of the commission.[116] In the long term, however, a policy of accommodation had to be backed by measures to contain Japanese expansionism. The most obvious expression of this determination was the effort directed towards the expansion of the Soviet armaments industry in an attempt to bolster frontier defences in the Far East.[117] In addition, assistance was provided to Chiang Kai-Shek in the belief that Chinese resistance to Japanese military adventures would divert attention away from the vulnerable Soviet borderlands.[118]

It was appreciated, however, that in order to restrain Japan, the Soviet Union needed to enlist the support of powerful allies in the Far East. A first step was taken in this direction in November 1933 with the establishment of diplomatic relations with the United States of America. In order to assuage American opinion, Litvinov pledged to halt the work of communist groups in the United States,[119] while in return Roosevelt agreed to defer the thorny question of the repayment of the debts incurred by the Tsarist regime for consideration at a later date.[120] Roosevelt's interest in the Far East, however, centred almost exclusively on the expansion of trade links,[121] and the eventual recovery of the Tsarist debts.[122] While Litvinov was anxious to foster economic ties with the United States,[123] to have accepted demands for the payment of wartime debts would have provoked similar representations from Britain and France.[124] The Soviet–American negotiations were finally abandoned in February 1935 with the reaffirmation by the Roosevelt administration of the decision incorporated in the Johnson Act of April 1934 to withhold credit facilities to those nations in default of payments on existing debts.[125]

In an attempt to resuscitate interest in Far Eastern security, Litvinov reverted to the promotion of an Eastern Locarno linking China, Japan, the Soviet Union and the United States in a security pact.[126] This proposal was put by Litvinov to the American Ambassador to Moscow, William C. Bullitt. Litvinov argued that

> anything that could be done to make the Japanese believe that the United States was ready to cooperate with Russia, even though there might be no basis for the belief, would be valuable.[127]

Bullitt replied that the United States would go no further than a reaffirmation of the decision taken in the Stimson Doctrine to deny recognition to territorial changes resulting from acts of aggression.[128] It was apparent, therefore, that despite the opening of American–Soviet negotiations Roosevelt had no intention of committing the United States to the containment of Japanese ambitions in China and Manchuria.

In assessing the Japanese menace, the Soviet government seemed to take seriously the vibrant nationalist challenge incorporated within the Tanaka Memorial of July 1927:

> It seems that the inevitability of crossing swords with Russia on the fields of Mongolia in order to gain possession of the wealth of North Manchuria is part of our programme of national development.[129]

The invasion of Manchuria in 1931 and the Japanese decision to quit the League of Nations in March 1933 underlined the nature of the growing threat to Soviet territorial integrity in the Far East. In response, while the Soviet Union remained reluctant to commit itself to an open-ended agreement on collective security, the need to enlist international support to defend the status quo in the Far East increasingly forced Litvinov to seek an improvement of relations with both the League of Nations and the United States. Yet the ambivalent nature of Soviet enthusiasm for collective security has been noted by Ulam:

> For the immediate and foreseeable future, the Soviet aims were not the punishment of aggressors or the preparation of a grand military alliance against them, but the non-involvement of the Soviet Union in war. Not a crusade against fascism, but the sensible objective of sparing their sorely tried country a military conflict they secretly realised it could not afford.[130]

If the storm clouds were gathering in Asia, difficulties were also being encountered in other spheres of interest. The lynchpin of Soviet foreign policy in Europe was the relationship established with the Weimar Republic.[131] In the political sphere the relationship had been based on the treaty of Rapallo concluded in April 1922 and further reinforced by the treaty of Berlin in April 1926.[132] The conclusion of these agreements united the two nations in an attempt to escape the restrictions imposed upon them by the balance of power created by the Versailles settlement. On a military level the alliance led to extensive collaboration between the Red Army and the Reichswehr in the field of armament production and the training of soldiers and airmen.[133] Economic links between the two states were actively promoted and flourished to the extent that, by 1932, Germany supplied approximately 45 per cent of all Soviet imports.[134] By 1932, however, there were signs that the importance assigned to the alliance by Germany was being progressively eroded.[135] Following the conclusion of the Locarno Pact and German entry into the League of Nations it seemed that German foreign policy, guided by Gustav Stresemann, was looking to establish ties with France and Britain. The lifting of the economic restrictions imposed on Germany by the Versailles settlement both encouraged Germany to look once again to links with the Western European community of nations and reduced the value of the post-war ties established with the Soviet Union.[136] E. H. Carr commented:

> What survived was a marriage of convenience which was kept up partly out of habit and partly because its advantages were still just great enough to warrant the effort required to maintain it.[137]

Undoubtedly this gradual diminution of the German–Soviet relationship was dramatically accelerated following Adolf Hitler's assumption of the post of Reichschancellor in January 1933.[138] The National Socialist Party added several new factors to the situation for, despite frequent declarations of friendship towards the Soviet Union, Hitler increasingly used the spectre of a communist threat to Western Europe and the role of Germany as a bulwark to repel communism, as a lever in his attempts to obtain a revision of the Versailles settlement. The portrayal of German interests as lying firmly with the Western European states in the fight against communism appeared to suggest that links with the Soviet Union were only of secondary importance. Furthermore, the advocation of the need for *Lebensraum,* actively promoted by the National Socialists, seemed to suggest that Germany must ultimately attempt to colonise large areas of the Soviet Union. In *Mein Kampf* Hitler had argued:

> We reverse the eternal Germanic migration to the South and to the West of Europe and look Eastwards.
>
> If we speak of new soil we can but think first of Russia and her subject border states.[139]

The implied threat to the future sovereignty of the Ukraine and the Caucasus was too implicit for the Soviet government to ignore. In addition, under Hitler's direction, the Nazi Party embarked on a rigorous campaign to decimate the political and physical strength of the German Communist Party. The extent of the violent campaign conducted against the German communists was carefully noted in Moscow.

Throughout 1933, however, the Soviet Union maintained its efforts to retain close links with Germany. In May 1933 *Izvestiya* proclaimed:

> in spite of their attitude towards Fascism, the people of the USSR wish to live in peace with Germany and consider that the development of German–Soviet relations is in the interests of both countries.[140]

In part this can be explained by the Soviet interpretation of the nature of fascism which paired fascism with social democracy:

> Objectively Social Democracy is the moderate wing of fascism.
>
> These organisations do not contradict but supplement one another. They are not antipodes but twins.
>
> Fascism is the shapeless political bloc of these two basic organisations, a bloc that has emerged in the post-war crisis of imperialism for the struggle against proletarian revolution.[141]

In this sense fascism did not present a new political phenomenon but rather a transitory stage in the decay of capitalism. Soviet fears were further reassured by the declaration of friendship contained in Hitler's first major speech on foreign policy delivered on 25 March 1933;[142] which Herman Goering reaffirmed in the same month: 'our own campaign for the extirpation of Communism in Germany has nothing to do with German–Russian relations';[143] and concluded that German–Soviet relations would 'remain as friendly as in former years'.[144]

Despite outward expressions of friendship, the Soviet–German relationship steadily deteriorated. A war of words conducted through the medium of the press was accompanied during 1933 by a decline in trade links and the termination of the relationship established between the Reichswehr and the Red Army.[145] In this context it was difficult for the Soviet leadership to avoid the conclusion that Hitler's Germany was no longer a trustworthy ally.[146] This opinion was seemingly underlined in March 1933 with the conclusion of the Four Power Pact, linking Britain, France, Germany and Italy in cooperation directed towards the maintenance of international peace. The agreement appeared to confirm the further reorientation of German policy away from the German–Soviet relationship.[147] German withdrawal from the League of Nations in October 1933 and the accent placed on military expansion only served to increase Soviet trepidation of ultimate German foreign policy goals. In order to illustrate the note of mistrust and suspicion that entered the German–Soviet relationship, Upham-Pope noted of Litvinov's discussions with von Neurath and Hitler, in Berlin in June 1934, that Litvinov

> let them know that, according to information in his possession,

Herr von Papen had offered an anti-Soviet pact to France in the summer of 1932, and, after France declined, in the summer of 1933 when Hitler was already in power, Rosenberg had been sent to London to try to induce England to sign an anti-Soviet pact. Neurath denied everything, but Litvinoff found nothing convincing in the denials.[148]

The first major admission of a serious breach in the façade of German–Soviet relations was contained in Litvinov's speech to the Central Executive Committee on 29 December 1933:

> in the past year our relations with Germany have become, it may be said, unrecognizable. In Germany speeches and declarations have been made, and incidents have occurred, which are not merely out of keeping with our former relations but rather give cause to think that they have been changed into their very opposite.[149]

Litvinov continued with an allusion to Nazi propaganda which he identified as designed

> not only to reconquer all the territories of which it [Germany] had been deprived by the Versailles treaty, not only to conquer lands where there was a German minority, but by fire and sword to cut a road for expansion in the East, which was not to stop at the Soviet frontier, and to enslave the Soviet peoples.[150]

Significantly Litvinov also spoke of Japanese intentions following the invasion of Manchuria:

> They have arrested the attention not only of our Union, but of the entire world, for Japanese policy is now the darkest cloud on the international horizon.[151]

With reference to the negotiations over the future of the Chinese Eastern Railway Litvinov noted:

> the more cool and patient our behaviour, the more insolent and provocative became the actions of the Japanese authorities in Manchuria. They gave the definite impression that they were deliberately trying to provoke us to stronger action than protests.
>
> . . . while the steps we are taking are for defensive purposes only, Japan, as you know, is feverishly preparing for war, and that can only be an offensive war, since nobody is threatening Japanese security.[152]

In outlining the need to respond to this dual threat, Litvinov declared:

> The ensuring of peace cannot depend on our efforts alone; it requires the collaboration and cooperation of other States. While

> therefore trying to establish and maintain friendly relations with all States, we are giving special attention to strengthening and making more close our relations with those which, like us, give proof of their sincere desire to maintain peace and are ready to resist those who break the peace.[153]

The central thesis in Litvinov's speech was the abandonment of the standpoint based purely on the division of international interests between capitalism and socialism. He was now anxious to present a distinction between the revisionist powers, which sought to obtain their goals through aggression and belligerency, and the bulk of the international community which, for various reasons, sought to defend the status quo and maintain peace.[154] Litvinov's references to Germany and Japan indicated that he saw them as the central forces within the former category. Furthermore, he sought to ally the Soviet Union with the United States of America, Britain, Italy and France in the preservation of international peace.[155] Litvinov identified the potential link between the powers defending the status quo as their common interest in fostering formal international cooperation:

> We have never rejected and do not reject organized international cooperation designed to consolidate peace. Not being doctrinaires, we do not refuse to use international associations or organisations, whether those already in existence or those which may be founded in the future, if we have or shall have reason to believe that they serve the cause of peace.[156]

Stalin had already suggested that the Soviet Union was being forced to reconsider its attitude to the League of Nations. In an interview for the *New York Times* on 25 December 1933, the Soviet leader commented:

> if the League were to turn out an obstacle, even if a small one, that made war more difficult, while it furthered, even to a small extent, the cause of peace, then we would not be against the League. If that is how things turn out, then it is not impossible that we shall support the League, notwithstanding its colossal defects.[157]

This tentative move towards formal collaboration with the League was essentially a response to the challenge presented by German and Japanese expansionism. The aim was to defuse the threat posed by the revisionist powers by establishing a network of alliances dedicated to maintaining the status quo. In the Far East steps had already been taken to find a counter to Japanese ambitions with the establishment of links with China and the United States of America. In Europe the task now was not only to prevent the creation of an anti-Bolshevik coalition, but also to contain the emerging challenge of German expansionism. In approaching this problem the Soviet Union increasingly found itself aligned with the various nations that sought to maintain the status quo either through the organs of the League of Nations or simply through traditional balance of power politics.[158]

In June 1930, in reply to a French proposal concerning the creation of a European federation of states, Stalin declared:

> The most striking representative of the bourgeois movement towards intervention against the Soviet Union is the bourgeois France of today, the fatherland of Pan-Europe, the cradle of the Kellogg Pact, the most aggressive and militaristic country, among all aggressive and militaristic countries of the world.[159]

This reaction was conditioned by the fact that at the Paris Peace Conference, in 1919, Clemenceau had taken a leading role in advocating either the destruction of the Bolshevik regime or its encirclement with a 'fil de fer barbels'.[160] In the decade following the conclusion of the war little had been done to repair the damage inflicted upon Franco–Soviet relations by French assistance to the White armies in Russia. Links between the two countries suffered a further setback in 1927 when the French Foreign Minister, Briand, admitted that the Treaty of Locarno was designed to draw Germany into the Western camp and disrupt ties between Berlin and Moscow:

> Une Allemagne resolument tournée vers l'Occident, en dépit de ses accords avec la Russie; une Allemagne qui a choisi, qui a compris enfin que son veritable intérêt etait de s'entendre avec les alliés et particulièrement avec la France.[161]

By the turn of the decade, however, growing French fears of a revival of German militarism forced a reconsideration of the stance adopted towards the Soviet Union. Some form of understanding now appeared relatively attractive not only in terms of defusing the bonds of German–Soviet solidarity but also in order to reinforce the network of alliances fostered by France in Eastern Europe.[162] The advancement of the relationship was assisted in 1931 by the Japanese invasion of Manchuria. With a mounting threat to its security in the Far East the Soviet Union displayed an active interest in securing its European frontiers. The result of this broad coalition of interests was the Franco–Soviet non-aggression pact of November 1932. The fact that this agreement was essentially designed to stabilise the situation in Eastern Europe was indicated by French insistence that it be preceded by similar pacts with Poland and Rumania, France's allies in Eastern Europe.[163]

In March 1933 the German Ambassador in Moscow reported to Berlin:

> the development of Soviet–French relations will be correlated with that of German–Soviet relations: the greater the cooling towards Germany, the greater the disposition to cordiality towards France.[164]

Indeed, the cooling of German–Soviet relations accelerated following the accession of Hitler to power despite the ratification, in May 1933, of a protocol extending the Treaty of Berlin and the signing of a German–Soviet trade protocol in March 1933.[165] Moscow's concern at the harassment of Soviet nationals in Germany and reports of German attempts to secure bilateral agreements with France, Britain and Poland undermined Soviet confidence in the sincerity of Hitler's declarations of friendship and cooperation.[166] The first outward emanation of this reorientation of attitude was the termination of Soviet–German military cooperation. Gerhard Weinberg noted:

> As these warnings and the friendly farewells to Germans who had run German military installations in the Soviet Union indicate, the Russians were still interested in co-operation, but under the circumstances Germany would have had to take the initiative in mending the fences. Any such step was precluded by Hitler's policy directives.[167]

Even before the German military instalations had been dismantled, the first French military advisers had arrived in the Soviet Union. In addition, in April 1933, France assigned, for the first time, a military attaché to its Moscow Embassy.[168] In July 1933 Litvinov visited Paris and in discussions with Paul-Boncour and Daladier the groundwork for the improvement of Franco–Soviet ties was established.[169] The negotiations had been given a significant boost when two months previously the French press had highlighted an article in *Pravda,* by Radek, declaring that the Soviet Union was firmly opposed to any suggestion of the revision of the Treaty of Versailles.[170] During the autumn of 1933 close contacts were maintained between the French Foreign Minister, Paul-Boncour, and the Soviet Ambassador to Paris, Dovgalevsky.[171] A further meeting between Paul-Boncour and Litvinov, in October 1933, followed the visit of the former French premier, Herriot, to Moscow in August and the despatch of a French delegation headed by the Minister for Air, Pierre Cot, to the Soviet Union in September 1933.[172] As a result of these contacts, on 28 December 1933, Paul-Boncour received a set of Soviet proposals that had been endorsed by the Politbureau on 19 December 1933:

> 1. The USSR agrees, under certain conditions, to join the League of Nations.

2. The USSR does not object to the conclusion, within the League of Nations, of a regional agreement on mutual defence from German aggression.
3. The USSR agrees that the following countries may be signatories to the agreement: Belgium, France, Czechoslovakia, Poland, Lithuania, Latvia, Estonia and Finland, or some of these countries, but that France and Poland, are under obligation to sign.
4. Negotiations on the precise definition of the commitments of a future convention on mutual defence can begin when France, as the initiator of the whole affair, submits a draft agreement.
5. Independent of commitments to the agreement on mutual defence, signatories to the agreement must also pledge to render each other diplomatic, moral and the possible material assistance in the event of a military attack not foreseen in the agreement itself, and also to exert appropriate influences in the press.[173]

During the following four months political instability within France, which led to the post of prime minister changing hands on three occasions, resulted in the proposals not being fully explored until April 1934 when the Foreign Minister, Louis Barthou, indicated that France was prepared to resume negotiations with the Soviet Union.[174] For both parties the need for some form of understanding had been emphasised by the conclusion of the German–Polish non-aggression pact of January 1934 which threatened to undermine the network of alliances negotiated by France in Eastern Europe.[175] Litvinov shared Barthou's concern at the growing German–Polish *rapprochement* which appeared to be based on their common determination to acquire vast tracts of the Ukraine. Furthermore, Litvinov was disturbed by the German determination to pursue bilateral agreements rather than conform to a system of collective security:

> Hitler needed this pact as a means of disrupting the ranks of the adherents of collective security and as an example to show that what Europe needed was *not* collective security but bilateral agreements. This enabled the German aggressor to decide for himself with whom, and when, to conclude agreements, and whom and when to attack. The German–Polish pact undoubtedly constituted the first breach in the edifice of collective security.[176]

In such a climate Litvinov turned increasingly to the League of Nations and the Disarmament Conference in an attempt to build a coalition capable of restraining the ambitions of the revisionist powers. Rather than supporting Germany in its attempts to prise concessions from Britain and France, Litvinov now urged Britain and France not to allow Germany's absence to block the progress of the Disarmament Conference. On 29 May 1934 Litvinov outlined his position to the conference:

> Could not the conference feel its way towards other guarantees for peace?
>
> Even if there should be dissident States that should by means prevent the remainder from coming still more closely together to take steps which would strengthen their own security.[177]

His fears concerning German ambitions in Eastern Europe were further fuelled in the same month when Soviet overtures for a Soviet–German protocol guaranteeing the independence of the Baltic states and Finland were rejected by Germany. By the summer of 1934, therefore, Litvinov was convinced that Soviet security interests lay firmly in some form of alliance with France which would stabilise the situation in Eastern Europe and deter German aggression when faced with the possibility of a war on two fronts.[178]

During the spring of 1934 Barthou visited Warsaw, Prague, Geneva, Bucharest and Belgrade to gauge the reaction to a Franco–Soviet alliance. As a result of these negotiations he proposed to Litvinov the creation of a pact of non-aggression and mutual assistance to be concluded between the Soviet Union, France, Poland, Czechoslovakia, Rumania and the Baltic states.[179] In addition, the Soviet Union was to become a member of the League of Nations and join Italy and Britain as guarantors of the Locarno Treaty. In essence, the pacts were designed to nullify German power in that the Nazi regime would be faced with the option of accepting the limitations imposed by collective security or face the prospect of diplomatic isolation. Barthou considered that Hitler would be forced to come to terms. As Weinberg noted:

> Germany could join a new multilateral system and perhaps rejoin the League as well — have its rearmament recognised by France, and be protected against attack from any neighbour; but the price was the renunciation of aggressive moves unless it were prepared to face a group of powers pledged to assist each other.[180]

Germany, however, refused the Franco–Soviet proposals for a system of collective security in Eastern Europe but more significantly Poland also declined to take part in the scheme:

> Warsaw was unwilling to undertake any obligations to help its neighbours militarily or to accept the help of any of them against another. Poland's policy precluded both aiding another power

> against either Germany or Russia and accepting military aid from one of them against the other.[181]

The Polish decision effectively destroyed Barthou's scheme for the creation of an eastern Locarno but could not temper the resolve of France and the Soviet Union to establish a formal alliance.

Soviet membership of the League was desirable not only to permit adherence to the Treaty of Locarno but also to symbolise the re-entry of the Soviet Union into the international community and its dedication to the cause of collective security. In order to achieve acceptance of the Soviet application it was important to enlist British support. After initial hesitation, when it became apparent that Germany had rejected proposals on collective security and disarmament, British policy swung firmly behind the Soviet candidacy.[182] The general debate on the Soviet application, however, was still heated and resulted in three motions opposing Soviet entry on the grounds that human rights were still extensively suppressed by the Soviet regime.[183] Greater issues, however, were at stake and, marshalled by Britain and France, the League Assembly welcomed Litvinov as he took his place on 18 September 1934. The only reservation Litvinov insisted upon was that the Soviet Union would not be required to submit to arbitration disputes that had occurred before its entry into the League of Nations. A further compromise was reached whereby Poland endorsed Soviet membership on condition that the Soviet Union agreed not to use the League as a vehicle for its campaign to reunite the Ukrainian and Byelorussian peoples under Soviet sovereignty.[184]

In his opening speech at Geneva Litvinov referred to the hostility and suspicion which had for so long characterised relations between the Soviet Union and the League of Nations:

> the people in the Soviet Union naturally feared that those nations united in the League might give collective expression to their hostility towards the Soviet Union and combine their anti-Soviet activities. It can hardly be denied that at that time, and even very much later, there were still statesmen who thought, or at least dreamed, of such collective action.
>
> For its part the Soviet Union . . . could not but observe the increasing activity in the League of Nations of states interested in the preservation of peace and their struggle against aggressive militaristic elements.
>
> I am . . . convinced that, with the firm will and close cooperation of all its members, a great deal could be done at any given moment for the utmost diminution of the danger of war. . . .
>
> The Soviet Government has never ceased working at this task throughout the whole period of its existence. It has come here to

combine its efforts with the efforts of other States represented in the League.[185]

The speech was a momentous occasion which marked a new departure in Soviet foreign policy and ended over a decade and a half of feuding between Moscow and Geneva.[186]

Soviet fears had originally been built on the assumption that the existence of the Soviet state was totally unacceptable to the western powers. It was the belief that the capitalist world would inevitably conspire physically to overthrow the challenge presented by communism which fuelled Soviet suspicion of the League of Nations for more than a decade. The decision to accept membership of the League represented a reorientation of Soviet foreign policy and was, in essence, a reaction to the challenge presented to Soviet territorial integrity by Hitler's Germany. It was ironic that it was largely the deterioration in Soviet–German relations which propelled the Soviet Union into the League for in the previous decade, in an attempt to prevent the creation of an anti-Bolshevik caucus in Europe, the Soviet Union had worked actively to forge links with Weimar Germany.[187] In essence it was a relationship based upon the recognition of a mutual interest in opposing Anglo–French domination of European affairs, and the desire to erode the limitations resulting from the Treaty of Versailles. While working comparatively smoothly during the 1920s the alliance later began to encounter problems. Max Beloff concluded:

> The fundamental change in Soviet foreign policy between 1929 and 1936 was in the relationship between Russia and Germany. The dynamic element in this change was clearly the German one — the transition from the Weimar Republic to the Third Reich. It was the aggressive potentialities of the latter which drove the Soviet Union to seek new guarantees for its security and, at the same time, made other countries less unwilling to enter into agreements with this hitherto outcast regime.[188]

The declining importance assigned by Berlin to the German–Soviet relationship had been evident even before the advent of the Third Reich. Faced with the prospect of a German nation determined to pursue an independent line in the field of foreign affairs the Soviet Union was forced to reassess its stance within the international system.[189] The realisation of the need to broaden the format of Soviet links with the major powers had been suggested in the latter half of the 1920s with the promotion of international trade agreements and Soviet participation on the Preparatory Commission on Disarmament convened under the aegis of the League of Nations at Geneva. The acquisition of an international platform for the Soviet viewpoint had been accompanied by a proportionate reduction in the activities of the Comintern which, in Trotsky's words, reduced the movement from the 'vanguards of world revolution' to the 'frontier guards' of the Soviet Union. The rise of the National Socialist movement within Germany and the spectre of Japanese militarism only served to accelerate this reorientation of policy. The counterweight to the threat presented by Germany and Japan was seen as an alliance with those elements which sought to maintain the status quò in international affairs. The essentially defensive character of this policy was illustrated by the measures taken by the Soviet Union in the Far East and Europe which centred on the cultivation of relations with France and the United States of America directed primarily towards the containment of German and Japanese nationalism.

The Soviet decision to join the League of Nations can only be viewed in the light of self-interest and, more particularly, in response to a challenge presented to future Soviet security. It only represented a positive contribution to the goals of disarmament and international cooperation in so far as they suited Soviet interests. In essence it represented an appreciation by the Soviet Union of the need to establish relations with the major world powers and, through the establishment of alliances and the mobilisation of collective security, to reinforce the measures already taken to increase the security of the Soviet Union. Theodore von Laue noted of Soviet foreign policy objectives: 'The principal one which overshadowed all others was to guarantee the absolute independence and security of the revolutionary development within its world base.'[190]

In addressing the Seventeenth Congress of the CPSU on 26 January 1934, at a time when Soviet policy was openly moving towards support of the League of Nations, Stalin declared: 'Our orientation in the past and our orientation at the present time is towards the USSR, and towards the USSR alone.'[191] For like the pacts of non-aggression with the Baltic states, the sale of the Chinese Eastern Railway to Manchukuo and the establishment of German–Soviet ties, the decision to join the League of Nations in September 1934 was conditioned by the traditional principles of self-interest and survival in what was considered to be a hostile environment. It barely concealed the suspicion and mistrust which still dominated relations between the Soviet Union and the outside world.

In one sense, however, it did represent a new departure in Soviet foreign policy. As Max Beloff noted:

> The position of the Soviet Union as an avowed centre of world revolutionary activity became less and less compatible with a diplomatic course which was directed towards ever closer relations with individual capitalist countries. The old dichotomy

between the two worlds had to be discarded in favour of a differentiation between the actively aggressive, the passively indifferent and the actively co-operative states.[192]

Soviet support for collective security and the recognition of the common challenge presented to the major powers by Germany and Japan heralded the widespread belief that cooperation within the League of Nations could result in the reintegration of the Soviet Union into the international community. Furthermore, it presented the opportunity to align the Soviet Union with the forces ostensibly defending international stability and the status quo. At a reception in Geneva, immediately following the admission of the Soviet Union into the League of Nations, a conversation was recorded between Barthou and Litvinov in which Barthou stated: 'I see a Russian general dancing with a virgin . . . or, let us say, with a somewhat damaged virgin. I am quite proud that I have played the role of matchmaker.'[193] Immediately taking up this allusion to the new relationship between the Soviet Union and the League of Nations, Litvinov replied: 'I will gladly dance with even a damaged virgin, if I know in which direction I dance.'[194] The prospects for the future, however, were not bright. Even the broad umbrella of the League of Nations was insufficient to absorb the absence of any real consensus on the format of international security and the role of the League of Nations. In this sense the value of the Soviet contribution was likely to be negligible. As Ian Grey concluded:

> The Soviet purpose of 'putting teeth into the Covenant' could make no headway when faith in the efficacy of the League was rapidly ebbing and suspicion of Soviet motives remained strong.[195]

Notes

1. Theodore H. von Laue, *Soviet Diplomacy: G. V. Chicherin, People's Commissar for Foreign Affairs, 1918-1930.* Quoted in Gordon A. Craig and Felix Gilbert, *The Diplomats 1919–1939.* Vol. 1: *The Twenties* (New York, 1972), pp. 235-9.
2. Jane Degras (ed.), *Soviet Documents on Foreign Policy.* Vol. 1: *1917–1924* (New York, 1978); Appeal from the People's Commissariat for Foreign Affairs to the toiling, oppressed, and exhausted peoples of Europe, 19 December 1917, pp. 18-21.
3. Richard F. Rosser, *An Introduction to Soviet Foreign Policy* (New Jersey, 1969), pp. 109-16.
4. Ibid., p. 124.

5. Degras, Appeal for the formation of the Communist International, 24 January 1919, pp. 136-7.
6. von Laue, p. 234.
7. Degras, Resolution of the Seventh Congress of the Russian Communist Party on the treaty of Brest-Litovsk, 8 March 1918, pp. 61-3.
8. Ian Grey, *The First Fifty Years, Soviet Russia 1917–1967* (London, 1967), pp. 252-3.
9. Lionel Kochan, *Russia and the Weimar Republic* (Cambridge, 1954), pp. 11-30.
10. Degras, Speech by Lenin to the Seventh Congress of the Russian Communist Party on the treaty of Brest-Litovsk, 7 March 1918, pp. 35-61. See also A. R. Peters, 'Russo–German Relations November 1914–March 1918', Sheffield City Polytechnic, Department of Political Studies Occasional Paper, Molotov–Ribbentrop Pact No. 2.
11. Degras, Speech by Lenin on Foreign Affairs to the Central Executive Committee, 14 May 1918, pp. 78-9.
12. Ibid.
13. D. S. Morris, R. H. Haigh and A. R. Peters, 'Prelude to Rapallo: Germany and Russia at Paris', Sheffield City Polytechnic, Department of Political Studies Occasional Paper, Molotov–Ribbentrop Pact No. 6.
14. F. P. Walters, *A History of the League of Nations* (London, 1969), p. 94.
15. Max Beloff, *The Foreign Policy of Soviet Russia.* Vol. 1: *1929–1936* (London, 1947), p. 42.
16. Fritz T. Epstein, *Russia and the League of Nations.* Quoted in Fritz T. Epstein, *Germany and the East* (Bloomington, Ind., 1973), p. 130.
17. David Lloyd George, *Memoirs of the Peace Conference,* Vol. 1 (London, 1938), p. 326.
18. Ibid., p. 377. See also ibid., Vol. II, p. 624.
19. Degras, Note from the People's Commissar for Foreign Affairs to President Wilson on intervention and the League of Nations, 24 October 1918, pp. 112-17.
20. Ibid., Reply by Chicherin to Lord Curzon's note on Russo–Polish relations, 17 July 1920, p. 195.
21. R. H. Haigh, D. S. Morris and A. R. Peters, 'Unhappy Landings', Sheffield City Polytechnic, Department of Political Studies Occasional Paper, Molotov–Ribbentrop Pact No. 7.
22. Kochan, pp. 30-5.
23. F. L. Schuman, *Soviet Politics* (London, 1948), p. 224.
24. Kochan, pp. 31-5; von Laue, p. 241.
25. G. Freund, *Unholy Alliance, Russo–German Relations from the Treaty of Brest-Litovsk to the Treaty of Berlin* (London, 1957), pp. 106-9.
26. Kochan, pp. 50-9.
27. Degras, Statement by Chicherin at the first plenary session of the Genoa Conference, 10 April 1922, pp. 298-301.
28. von Laue, p. 244.

29. Schuman, p. 225.
30. Beloff, pp. 43-4.
31. Freund, pp. 108-39.
32. George F. Kennan, *Soviet Foreign Policy, 1917–1941* (Princeton, N.J., 1960), p. 47.
33. Degras, Resolution of the Ninth Congress of the Russian Communist Party on relations with the capitalist world, 16 March 1921, p. 236.
34. Grey, p. 253.
35. Freund, pp. 110-18.
36. von Laue, p. 269.
37. Grey, pp. 255-6.
38. Degras, Report by Chicherin to the Central Executive Committee on foreign relations, 18 October 1924, pp. 460-9.
39. Walters, p. 102.
40. Ibid., p. 164.
41. Kochan, pp. 52-4.
42. Walters, p. 167.
43. Ibid., p. 232.
44. Degras, Report by Chicherin to the Central Executive Committee on foreign relations, 18 October 1924, pp. 460-9.
45. Ibid.
46. Beloff, p. 134.
47. Walters, pp. 103-10; also pp. 95-7.
48. Ibid., p. 265.
49. Degras, p. 464.
50. Ibid., pp. 79, 130, 139.
51. Jane Degras (ed.), *Soviet Documents on Foreign Policy*. Vol. 2: *1925–1932* (New York, 1978), Press statement by Litvinov on the Soviet Union and the League of Nations, 23 November 1925, pp. 64-6.
52. Walters, pp. 354-5.
53. Kochan, pp. 101-19.
54. Ibid., pp. 31-5.
55. Isaac Deutscher, *Stalin, A Political Biography* (Harmondsworth, 1977), pp. 388-9.
56. von Laue, p. 272.
57. Ibid.
58. Deutscher, pp. 387-90.
59. Grey, p. 260.
60. Deutscher, p. 389.
61. Kochan, pp. 31-5.
62. von Laue, p. 262.
63. Deutscher, p. 399.
64. Grey, pp. 262-4; Schuman, p. 227.
65. Jane Degras (ed.), *Soviet Documents on Foreign Policy*. Vol. 3: *1933–1941* (New York, 1978), pp. 45-6. Interview between Stalin and Duranty of the *New York Times* on the Soviet attitude to the League of Nations, 25 December 1933.

66. Degras, Vol. 2, Extracts from the Report of Rykov, Chairman of the Council of People's Commissars, to the Fourth Soviet Congress, 18 April 1927, pp. 182-92.
67. von Laue, p. 277.
68. Deutscher, p. 400.
69. von Laue, p. 278.
70. Arthur Upham-Pope, *Maxim Litvinov* (London, 1943), pp. 224-5.
71. Henry L. Roberts, *Maxim Litvinov,* quoted in Gordon A. Craig and Felix Gilbert, *The Diplomats 1919–1939.* Vol. 2: *The Thirties* (New York, 1977), p. 347.
72. Walters, pp. 370-6.
73. Upham-Pope, pp. 244-50.
74. Ibid., p. 251.
75. Walters, pp. 370-3.
76. Beloff, p. 45.
77. Degras, Vol. 2, Press statement by Litvinov on his appointment as Commissar for Foreign Affairs, 25 July 1930, pp. 449-51.
78. Beloff, p. 46.
79. von Laue, pp. 278-81.
80. Louis Fischer, *Men and Politics* (New York, 1941), p. 147.
81. Roberts, p. 344.
82. Walters, pp. 440-1.
83. Ibid., pp. 440-2.
84. Degras, Vol. 2, Press statement by Litvinov on his departure from Geneva before the final session of the Preparatory Commission on Disarmament, and on his visit to Milan, 27 November 1930, pp. 462-4.
85. Ibid., Report by Rykov, Chairman of the Council of People's Commissars to the Fifth Soviet Congress, 22 May 1929, pp. 364-79.
86. Grey, p. 259; Schuman, pp. 232-3.
87. Degras, Vol. 2, Press statement by Litvinov on his appointment as Commissar for Foreign Affairs, 25 July 1930, pp. 449-51.
88. Schuman, p. 232.
89. Beloff, p. 42.
90. Degras, Vol. 2, p. 450.
91. Beloff, pp. 43-4.
92. Ibid., p. 44.
93. Roberts, Speech by Litvinov to Disarmament Conference, 11 February 1932, pp. 350-1.
94. Walters, pp. 500-3.
95. Ibid., p. 502.
96. Ibid., p. 503.
97. Ibid., pp. 370-6.
98. Ibid., pp. 511-12.
99. Ibid., pp. 512-15.
100. Ibid.
101. Roberts, p. 351.
102. Grey, p. 261.
103. Roberts, pp. 351-2.

104. Hermann Mau and Helmut Krausnick, *German History 1933–1945* (New York, 1963), pp. 61-2.
105. Walters, pp. 543-4.
106. Beloff, p. 53.
107. Walters, pp. 504-5.
108. Schuman, pp. 229-36.
109. Ibid., p. 235.
110. Grey, p. 263.
111. Upham-Pope, p. 274.
112. Ibid., p. 275.
113. Schuman, p. 239.
114. Beloff, p. 79.
115. Schuman, p. 237.
116. Ibid.
117. Kennan, p. 76.
118. Beloff, pp. 85-8.
119. Adam B. Ulam, *Expansion and Coexistence. The History of Soviet Foreign Policy 1917–1967* (London, 1968), p. 213.
120. Grey, pp. 265-6.
121. Upham-Pope, p. 281.
122. Beloff, pp. 119-20. See also Donald G. Bishop, *The Roosevelt–Litvinov Agreements. The American View* (New York, 1965).
123. Ulam, pp. 211-15.
124. Thomas A. Bailey, *A Diplomatic History of the American People* (New Jersey, 1974), pp. 671-2.
125. Schuman, pp. 227-41.
126. Ulam, p. 214.
127. Ibid.
128. Ibid., p. 215.
129. Schuman, p. 243. Reprinted from *The China Critic,* 24 September 1921.
130. Ulam, p. 217.
131. Deutscher, pp. 403-4.
132. Freund, pp. 233-44.
133. A. R. Peters, R. H. Haigh and D. S. Morris, 'Russo–German Military Collaboration 1921–1933', Sheffield City Polytechnic, Department of Political Studies Occasional Paper, Molotov–Ribbentrop Pact No. 5.
134. Beloff, p. 96.
135. Freund, pp. 246-7. See also W. Hoffding, 'German trade with the Soviet Union', *Slavonic Review* (1936–37), Vol. XIV, pp. 473-94.
136. Kochan, pp. 152-66.
137. E. H. Carr, *German–Soviet Relations Between the Two World Wars, 1919–1936* (Baltimore, 1951), p. 101.
138. Kochan, pp. 167-72.
139. Schuman, p. 242.
140. Beloff, p. 97.
141. Deutscher, p. 401.

142. Gerhard L. Weinberg, *The Foreign Policy of Hitler's Germany. Diplomatic Revolution in Europe 1933–1936* (London, 1970), p. 78.
143. Carr, p. 109.
144. Ibid.
145. G. H. Stein, 'Russo–German Collaboration: The Last Phase, 1933', *Political Science Quarterly,* Vol. LXXVII (March 1962), pp. 54-71.
146. Deutscher, pp. 408-9.
147. Carr, pp. 114-15.
148. Upham-Pope, p. 337.
149. Degras, Vol. 3, Speech by Litvinov on foreign affairs to the Central Executive Committee, 29 December 1933, pp. 48-60.
150. Ibid.
151. Ibid.
152. Ibid.
153. Ibid.
154. Beloff, p. 93.
155. Degras, Vol. 3, pp. 48-60.
156. Ibid.
157. Degras, Vol. 3, Interview between Stalin and Duranty of the *New York Times* on the Soviet attitude to the League of Nations, 25 December 1933, p. 45.
158. Deutscher, p. 409.
159. Degras, Vol. 2, Extracts from Stalin's report to the Sixteenth Congress of the Communist Party of the Soviet Union, 27 June 1930, pp. 441-7.
160. Arnold Wolfers, *Britain and France between Two Wars* (New York, 1966), p. 132.
161. Ibid., p. 134.
162. Ibid., p. 135.
163. Upham-Pope, pp. 275-6.
164. Stein, p. 59.
165. Beloff, p. 96.
166. Weinberg, p. 78.
167. Ibid., p. 82.
168. Ibid., p. 79.
169. Wolfers, pp. 136-7.
170. Ibid.
171. Beloff, p. 138.
172. I. K. Koblyakov, *USSR: For Peace against Aggression 1933–1941* (Moscow, 1976), p. 47.
173. Ibid., pp. 44-8.
174. Koblyakov, p. 48.
175. Weinberg, p. 180.
176. Koblyakov, p. 51.
177. Roberts, p. 354.
178. Deutscher, pp. 408-10.
179. Wolfers, pp. 136-7.
180. Weinberg, p. 183.
181. Ibid., p. 184.

182. Upham-Pope, pp. 337-8.
183. Schuman, pp. 254-5.
184. Walters, pp. 579-85.
185. Degras, Vol. 3, Litvinov's speech at the League Assembly on the entry of the USSR into the League of Nations, 18 September 1934, pp. 89-96.
186. Beloff, p. 42.
187. Freund, pp. 245-50.
188. Beloff, p. 56.
189. Kochan, pp. 138-51.
190. von Laue, p. 279.
191. Degras, Vol. 3, Extracts from a report by Stalin to the Seventeenth Congress of the CPSU, 26 January 1934, pp. 65-72.
192. Beloff, p. 93.
193. Upham-Pope, p. 351.
194. Ibid.
195. Grey, p. 268.

2 Defending the League

On 10 September 1934 the Soviet Union formally accepted membership of the League of Nations. In his first speech before the League Assembly Maxim Litvinov, the Soviet Commissar for Foreign Affairs, acknowledged the problems that had beset relations between the Soviet Union and the League of Nations:

> the relations between the Soviet State and the League of Nations could not be other than those existing between itself and the States belonging to the League. Not only this, but the people in the Soviet Union naturally feared that these nations united in the League might give collective expression to their hostility towards the Soviet Union and combine their anti-Soviet activities. It can hardly be denied that at the time, and even very much later, there were still statesmen who thought, or at least dreamed, of such collective action.[1]

Litvinov continued by outlining his conviction that international stability was under threat:

> many believed that the spirit of war might be exorcised by adjurations, resolutions and declarations. Now everybody knows that the exponents of the idea of war, the open promulgators of the refashioning of the map of Europe and Asia by the sword, are not to be intimidated by paper obstacles. Members of the League of Nations knew this by experience. We are now confronted with the task of averting war by more effective means.[2]

As a contribution to this goal the Soviet Commissar declared:

> The Soviet Government has never ceased working at this task throughout the whole period of its existence. It has come here to combine its efforts with the efforts of other States represented in the League.[3]
>
> I am . . . convinced that, with the firm will and close co-operation of all its members, a great deal could be done at any given moment for the utmost diminution of the danger of war.[4]

As early as 29 December 1933, in an address to the Central Executive Committee, Litvinov had conceded that it was pointless to analyse international relations purely on the basis of a division of interests between the capitalist and socialist outlooks. He argued that a distinction should be made between the revisionist powers which sought to obtain their goals through aggression and belligerency and the bulk of the international community which, for various reasons, sought to defend the status quo and maintain peace.[5] The Soviet Commissar indicated that he saw Germany and Japan as the central forces in the revisionist camp. Furthermore, he argued, only a cursory examination of the policies being pursued by the two nations suggested that both aspired to detach large areas of territory from the Soviet Union. Litvinov continued with an allusion to Nazi propaganda which apparently aimed

> not only to reconquer all the territories of which it [Germany] had been deprived by the Versailles Treaty, not only to conquer lands where there was a German minority, but by fire and sword to cut a road for expansion in the East, which was not to stop at the Soviet frontier, and to enslave the Soviet peoples.[6]

With reference to Japanese activity in Manchuria, Litvinov noted:

> They have arrested the attention not only of our Union, but of the entire world, for Japanese policy is now the darkest cloud on the international horizon.[7]
>
> while the steps we are taking are for defensive purposes only, Japan, as you know, is feverishly preparing for war and that can only be an offensive war, since nobody is threatening Japanese security.[8]

In outlining the need to respond to this dual threat Litvinov continued:

> The ensuring of peace cannot depend on our efforts alone; it requires the collaboration and co-operation of other States. While therefore trying to establish and maintain friendly relations with all States, we are giving special attention to strengthening and making more close our relations with those which, like us,

give proof of their sincere desire to maintain peace and are ready to resist those who break the peace.[9]

The logical extension of this line of reasoning was that the Soviet Union should align its policy with the nations apparently dedicated to maintaining the status quo and seeking to contain German and Japanese ambitions under the banner of collective security and the League of Nations. Stalin had confirmed this reorientation of strategy in an interview given in December 1933 in which he had argued that 'notwithstanding its colossal defects' the League of Nations was worthy of support if it could contribute effectively to the prevention of war.[10]

Considering the threat perceived by the Soviet Union from Germany and Japan it appeared logical for the Soviet Union to embrace the League of Nations. Furthermore, in order to alleviate suspicion of Soviet motives, Litvinov elected to take an active part in the proceedings at Geneva. Within three months of joining the League Litvinov had accepted arbitration by the League in a dispute between the Soviet Union and Uruguay, and had agreed to observe an embargo imposed upon the export of arms to Bolivia and Paraguay. In December 1934 Litvinov further reinforced the image of the Soviet Union as an advocate of international stability by joining Britain and France in condemning the assassination of King Alexander of Yugoslavia and by lending his support to the British scheme to establish an international police force to supervise the plebiscite on the future status of Saar.[11]

Yet to suggest that the accession of the Soviet Union to the League of Nations marked the establishment of close ties between Moscow, Paris and London would be largely incorrect. The Soviet regime was only too aware of the shortcomings of the League of Nations. While accepting membership of the League on 18 September 1934, Litvinov declared his concern for the structure and authority of the organisation:

> Far be it from me to overrate the opportunities and means of the League of Nations for the organisation of peace. I realise, better perhaps than any of you, how limited these means are. I am aware that the League does not possess the means for the complete abolition of war.[12]

This point was re-emphasised by Molotov in his report to the Seventh Soviet Congress on 28 January 1935:

> Since the League of Nations may now play a certain positive part in maintaining peace the Soviet Union could not but admit the expediency of collaborating with the League of Nations in this

matter, although we are not prone to overestimate the importance of such organisations.[13]

Molotov indicated that the Soviet Union sought a period of peace and tranquillity. Within this context international cooperation and the pursuit of collective security were of mutual interest to both the Soviet Union and the League of Nations.[14]

If, however, the Soviet Union saw the League primarily as a vehicle to satisfy its immediate need for security and stability there were also indications that the western powers were divided in their perceptions of the value to be assigned to links with Moscow. Although Soviet candidature had been promoted by both Britain and France, it was evident that British enthusiasm for the opening of links with the Soviet Union at no time matched the declarations of friendship and solidarity emanating from the French government. While Britain had formally recognised the Soviet regime in 1924 and had signed an Anglo–Soviet trade agreement in April 1930, relations between the two nations had been continually hampered by mistrust and barely concealed hostility.[15] The relationship was further soured in April 1933 with the trial of six British engineers working for the Metropolitan-Vickers Company installing turbines for the Soviet regime. The six engineers were accused of sabotage, a charge which prompted Sir John Simon, the British Foreign Secretary, to inform the House of Commons:

> The main accusations were palpably absurd, because in so far as they were an accusation that these men were engaged in what is called the Secret Service, I have said at this Box that it was not true; and in so far as they were an accusation that these engineers were engaged in deliberately wrecking their engineering plant, you might as well accuse Mr Speaker of deliberately breaking the windows of the House of Commons.[16]

Despite the element of discord that existed between London and Moscow, Sir John Simon was prepared to concede that the Franco–Soviet proposals for a regional security agreement in Eastern Europe based on non-aggression and mutual assistance were a valuable contribution to European stability. Simon emphasised, however, that Britain had no intention of involving itself in an alliance with any of the East European nations. The Foreign Secretary informed the House of Commons on 13 July 1934:

> We made it entirely plain from the beginning whatever may be the interest or encouragement which this country may be prepared to offer to this new pact, we are not undertaking any new obligations at all. That is quite clear and definitely understood, and there is no possible question or challenge about it.[17]

> this is not a case in which we are extending our own commitments in any way whatever.[18]

This assumption was based on the premise that Britain must avoid military or political entanglements in Eastern Europe. As early as 16 February 1925, the British Foreign Secretary, Austen Chamberlain, had outlined the dangers of providing military guarantees in areas of the world which were not of vital significance to British interests:

> A form of guarantee which is so general that we undertake exactly the same obligations in defence, shall I say of the Polish Corridor (for which no British Government ever will or ever can risk the bones of a British grenadier) as we extend to these international arrangements or conditions on which, as our history shows, our national existence depends, is a guarantee so wide and general that it carries no conviction whatever and gives no sense of security to those who are concerned in our action.[19]

The conviction that Britain should avoid direct involvement in East European affairs was reinforced by a general feeling that, as a result of the Versailles settlement, Germany had legitimate grievances worthy of redress in an area of Europe that had traditionally been considered a German sphere of interest. In addressing the House of Commons on 6 February 1934, Sir John Simon tacitly admitted that the Versailles Treaty had denied Germany certain rights and that this position could not be expected to persist indefinitely:

> Germany's claim to equality of rights ought not to be resisted. There is little likelihood of peace in the world if you try to put one country or one race under an inferior jurisdiction.[20]

The logic of appeasement was further fuelled by those who maintained an implicit faith in the 'reasonable' nature of German claims. In January 1933, on returning from a visit to Germany where he had spoken with Hitler, Lord Lothian wrote to *The Times:*

> National Socialism . . . is a movement of individual and national self respect. . . . The central factor in Europe today is that Germany does not want war and is prepared to renounce it absolutely as a method of settling disputes with her neighbours, provided she is given equality.
>
> I have not the slightest doubt that his [Hitler's] attitude is perfectly sincere.[21]

In this light the British government was only too willing to adopt a conciliatory line, following Germany's withdrawal from the Disarmament Conference in the hope that, once certain grievances had been recognised, Germany would be prepared to enter into a general

European security settlement. This stance was reflected in the format of the communiqué issued following the Anglo–French discussions held in London on 1-3 February 1935. The communiqué outlined Anglo–French opposition to any attempt by Germany to abrogate the armament levels established by the Versailles Treaty: 'neither Germany nor any other power whose armaments have been defined by the Peace Treaties is entitled by unilateral action to modify these obligations.'[22] The central theme, however, was the suggestion that rearmament might be accepted if it was part of a wider security agreement:

> nothing would contribute more to the restoration of confidence and the prospects of peace among nations than a general settlement freely negotiated between Germany and the other powers.[23]

Clearly the pursuit of some form of understanding with Germany played a prominent role in the formulation of British foreign policy in this period. Therefore, despite the flagrant violation of the Versailles Treaty presented on 16 March 1935, by the announcement that Germany intended to reintroduce conscription in order to establish an army of 36 divisions, it was apparent that Sir John Simon had no intention of allowing an opportunity to engineer an agreement with Hitler to escape his grasp. Of the conversations which took place between the Foreign Secretary and Hitler in Berlin in March 1935, Anthony Eden subsequently recorded:

> Simon put the case for an Eastern Pact of mutual assistance comprising the governments of eastern Europe, on the model of Locarno. But it was soon clear that Hitler would have none of it and preferred individual non-aggression pacts. . . .
>
> Hitler told us that war between Germany and Czechoslovakia could be excluded, because there was an arbitration agreement, and assured us that Germany would never declare war on Russia. He denounced Moscow's policies and said that the Russian desire for an Eastern Pact was in order to have a freer hand in the Far East.[24]

In his report to London, Simon concluded:

> The practical result of our Berlin visit is to establish that Germany greatly desires a good understanding with Britain, but that she is determined to go her own course in rearmament; that she expects in time to get all Germans within her borders, including Austria; that she does not fear isolation and has no intention of joining in collective security.[25]

It appeared vital, therefore, to gain German agreement to a European security pact before Hitler felt sufficiently confident to extract an exorbitant price. In an attempt to clear the obstacles to further negotiation the British government agreed to explore means by which Germany could be permitted to rearm and also possibly secure the return of former colonial possessions.[26] Given Hitler's stated aversion to an East European pact of mutual assistance, British attention focused increasingly on the proposals for a West European air pact.[27] In this context the prospect of a Franco–Soviet alliance was relegated to a matter of secondary importance. Indeed the British Foreign Secretary appeared to place little faith in any form of alliance with the Soviet Union:

> We may see the curious spectacle of British Tories collaborating with Russian Communists, while the League of Nations thunders applause. There may be no other course, but will it ensure peace? I most gravely doubt it.[28]

It appeared, therefore, that the British government was prepared to welcome the Franco–Soviet pact only in so far as it was compatible with the Covenant of the League of Nations and the Treaty of Locarno, and did not involve Britain in a precise military commitment to East European stability. The pact was seen as a means of pacifying French fears for the future stability of Eastern Europe. With this achieved it was hoped that Paris might adopt a more conciliatory approach to the problem of reaching an understanding with Germany in Western Europe.[29]

The Franco–Soviet pact was finally signed on 2 May 1935, and was followed on 16 May by a similar pact of mutual assistance concluded between the Soviet Union and Czechoslovakia. Although the agreement fell short of the original design for a regional security arrangement, it did apparently succeed in linking France and its East European allies with the Soviet Union. In the presence of the French Foreign Minister, Pierre Laval, Litvinov declared:

> I trust that the signature of the pact will be not the culmination but the beginning of collaboration between the Soviet Union and the French Republic, still closer and more beneficial, to secure for all nations tranquil development in conditions of unbroken peace.[30]

To conclude, however, that the signing of the pact represented the establishment of an understanding between France and the Soviet Union on the format of European affairs would be misleading. As early as 12 February 1934, the State Secretary to the German Foreign Ministry, Bulow, in a despatch to the German Ambassador in

Moscow, Nadolny, had cast doubts on the strength of the Franco–Soviet alliance:

> we are convinced that the trees of the Franco–Russian afforestation will not reach the sky and we therefore do not wish to rush into expense in order to drain off their waters.
>
> In any case the Russo–French *rapprochement* must not intimidate us; it cannot lead very far or become really dangerous to us.[31]

This same note of scepticism was discernible in a despatch to the German Foreign Ministry by Count Werner von der Schulenburg, Nadolny's successor in Moscow, following the signing of the pact:

> [the agreement's] extremely cautious and elaborate language does not give the impression of two partners wishing to bind themselves to one another at all costs. On the contrary, one could if one were so minded infer from the very text of the Treaty and the attached Protocol that France at least has left herself a good many loopholes.[32]

The loopholes Schulenburg referred to concerned three areas of the agreement. First, on French insistence, the provisions for mutual assistance were tied exclusively to reaction against an unprovoked attack on either state by another European nation. The terms of the pact thus explicitly ruled out the possibility of France being drawn into a war between the Soviet Union and Japan.[33] Secondly, it was agreed that the pact would be framed with reference to the provisions of the League of Nations and be based on the execution of Articles 10 and 16 of the Covenant. Although the decision to implement the pact did not rest irrevocably with the Council of the League of Nations, the arrangement did ensure that an attempt to enforce the pact would have to be considered initially by the machinery of the League of Nations. In paragraph 2 of the protocol further restrictions were imposed on the implementation of the agreement with the tacit understanding that the pact was to be aligned with the Treaty of Locarno.[34] In this context the decision to denounce a German act in Western Europe as aggression lay not with France but with Britain and Italy as guarantors of the Locarno agreement. Finally, the pact did not contain provisions for the establishment of relations between Soviet and French military personnel. Given the obvious need to establish contingency plans if assistance was to be rendered in the event of aggression, this omission was particularly significant for it tacitly admitted the problems presented by the ultra-defensive strategy of the French army in the post-war era and the geographical barrier between the Soviet Union and Germany presented by Poland and the Baltic states.[35]

In attempting to account for the tentative, almost half-hearted, nature of the pact, it has to be admitted that the problems surrounding the provision of military assistance were immense given the defensive posture adopted by French military strategists and the hostility of Poland, Rumania and the Baltic states to the passage of the Red Army through their territory. In addition, France feared that military alignment with the Soviet Union would alienate many of its Eastern European allies who, in their fear of the Soviet Union, might turn to Germany for protection.[36] As Arnold Wolfers noted:

> It was very doubtful from the point of French security whether promises of Soviet military assistance, even if they could be relied upon, could compensate France for the loss of her lesser military allies in Central Europe to the German camp.[37]

Throughout the negotiation of the pact the British government, with its traditional distaste for commitments in Eastern Europe, had attempted to restrain the French from entering into a full-scale military agreement with the Soviet Union. Wolfers summarised the situation in the following terms:

> France seeking to incorporate into her system of defences as many of the Slavic powers to the east of Germany as she believed at a given time necessary for her security; Britain trying to dissociate herself as long as possible and to draw France back from the 'danger zone' of Eastern Europe.[38]

It would appear, however, that French doubts as to the value of the pact went far deeper than the aspersions cast upon its worth by the British. Louis Fischer has argued that 'The central factor which conduced to French acceptance of the mutual defence treaty with Russia was psychological rather than strategic.'[39] As early as November 1933 the French Ambassador to Moscow, Charles Alphand, had outlined the barrier that existed between the Soviet Union and the rest of Europe:

> I do not believe that the Soviets agree to bind themselves in a concrete manner with any capitalist state. . . . The question is not one of alliance, which I do not consider materially possible under the present circumstances.[40]

This suspicion of Soviet sincerity might serve to explain the lack of attention given to the military aspect of the Franco–Soviet pact. The value of the pact lay in the desire to break the bonds of German–Soviet *rapprochement* which had grown out of the Treaty of Rapallo.

The pact represented an opportunity to isolate Germany politically and militarily in Eastern and Western Europe. In April 1936 Alphand concluded:

> The chief interest of the alliance with Russia is to establish this force on our side and to prevent it from being on the side of our enemies. Moreover I persist in considering that the chief means of collaboration with the USSR in the case of war would be the support given to our allies in the way of equipment, provisions, raw materials and munitions, to the extent that this would seem necessary to these allies themselves.[41]

It would seem, therefore, that the main thrust of French foreign policy focused on the need to contain the threat perceived by resurgent German nationalism. This was indicated by the format of the Anglo–French communiqué of 3 February 1935, and the tone of the Stresa Conference of April 1935, which stressed the need to concentrate on the attainment of a comprehensive European security arrangement. In this context the Franco–Soviet pact was simply a bargaining card in the wider game of European diplomacy. Laval had no intention of committing France irrevocably to the defence of the Soviet Union. To have accepted such an alignment would have seriously curtailed his hopes for a Franco–German understanding.[42] The delaying tactics pursued by Laval in the period prior to the signing of the pact reinforced the suspicion that the opening of a dialogue with Germany was still the central objective of French diplomacy.[43]

That Laval was forced to abandon his delaying tactics and finally sign the Franco–Soviet pact in May 1935 was indicative of growing Soviet concern at the Anglo–French attempts to reach an agreement with Germany. In an official reply to the Anglo–French proposals for a European settlement the Soviet government, on 20 February 1935, alluded to the dangers of seeking a purely Western European agreement:

> the only way of attaining the object put forward at the London meeting of 'organising security in Europe' is through the realisation of all the regional pacts and agreements mentioned in the London communiqué, and that . . . neglect of one or the other of these agreements will only not serve 'to strengthen the prospects of peace', but is likely to be regarded as open encouragement to break the peace in the area in question.[44]

The following month, during the visit of a British minister to Moscow, Stalin emphasised the need to ensure that a network of regional pacts of mutual assistance was concluded. Eden noted:

> Stalin said that German diplomacy was generally clumsy, but maintained that the only way to meet the present situation was by some scheme of pacts. Germany must be made to realise that if she attacked any other nation she would have Europe against her.[45]

The signing of the Franco–Soviet pact was, therefore, a significant triumph for Soviet diplomacy. Adam B. Ulam concluded:

> The importance of the treaty lay precisely in the fact that it blocked, in so far as any written guarantee could block, the first phase of the German attempt to gain a free hand against the USSR.
>
> . . . the possibility of western support could no longer be excluded from German calculations. If Hitler's whole anti-Communist stance was an attempt to isolate the USSR diplomatically and make sure that Germany could deal with her at her leisure, then the Franco–Soviet agreement was a resounding defeat for that policy and propaganda.[46]

The signing of the pact and Soviet membership of the League of Nations seemed to suggest that Stalin had abandoned the policy fostered by the Treaty of Rapallo in 1922 and that Soviet policy was now firmly aligned with Britain and France. This conclusion was supported by the rapid deterioration of German–Soviet relations that followed the establishment of the National Socialist regime in Germany.[47] In an interview, which was reprinted in the *Daily Telegraph* on 10 May 1935, Hitler made his attitude to the Franco–Soviet pact perfectly clear:

> We are ready, and always have been, to sign any document whose full requirements can be foreseen and whose clear aim is peace. We will sign non-aggression pacts with all the world, but we will not sign a multilateral pact of mutual assistance in the East.
>
> In no circumstances would Germany fight for the Bolsheviks. Rather than sign such a Pact I would hang myself.[48]

In addition, it was apparent that Hitler saw Eastern Europe as a German sphere of interest. Gerhard Weinberg subsequently noted:

> He intended to take as much territory as he could and as soon as possible and he was of the opinion that the rule of the Communists in Russia was advantageous for Germany in that it simultaneously weakened Russia's powers of resistance and provided him with an excellent basis for propaganda inside and outside Germany.[49]

Initially, Stalin adopted a cautious approach to the new German regime based outwardly on the ideological conviction that fascism was a transitory phenomenon, but also on the assumption that the value of military and economic ties would continue to bind the two nations together.[50] Yet, following Rosenberg's mission to London in May 1933, and Hugenberg's address to the World Economic Conference in June 1933, the determination of Germany to colonise vast tracts of Eastern Europe could not be ignored by the Soviet leadership.[51] In such a climate relations deteriorated rapidly. The decision in the summer of 1933 to cancel German military facilities within the Soviet Union appeared to symbolise the end of the *rapprochement* established by the Treaty of Rapallo. Although Hitler did not seek to cut all links with the Soviet Union, relations were to be severely curtailed. A German Foreign Ministry memorandum, dated 26 September 1933 outlined the German leader's thoughts on the format of relations with Moscow:

> a restoration of the German–Russian relationship would be impossible because the new order in Germany had crushed every hope the Russians had to carry out the world revolution.
>
> A sharp antagonism would of course remain between Germany and Russia but he was not in favour of our side breaking off German–Russian relations or furnishing the Russians with a pretext for such a break.
>
> We ought not, however, to indulge in delusions. The Russians were always lying and they would one day leave us in the lurch.[52]

In his report to the Seventeenth Congress of the CPSU on 26 January 1934, Stalin alluded to the apparent change in German foreign policy. He referred to a 'new' policy

> which, in the main, recalls the policy of the German Kaiser, who at one time occupied the Ukraine, marched against Leningrad and converted the Baltic countries into a *place d'armes* for this march; and this 'new' policy is obviously gaining the upper hand.[53]

The cooling of German–Soviet relations was further compounded by the signing of the German–Polish pact of non-aggression in January 1934. In April 1934 the German Foreign Ministry rejected Soviet overtures for a joint guarantee of the Baltic states, a decision which provoked the resignation of the German Ambassador to Moscow, Nadolny, who had worked to revive Soviet–German relations.[54] It was, therefore, in an atmosphere of growing anxiety, following the German refusal to endorse a system of collective security in Eastern Europe in preference to bilateral pacts of non-aggression, that the

Soviet Union turned to France as a counterweight to German ambitions. Gerhard Weinberg concluded:

> There is considerable evidence . . . that the continued worry of Soviet leaders about German intentions led them to hope that there was still some prospect of normalising political relations. The Soviet Union entered upon its new treaty with France reluctantly and while still leaving open other possibilities. Soviet leaders repeatedly indicated as much to the Germans by expressions of fear of German intentions combined with hope for new agreements.[55]

The remaining link in the relationship between Germany and the Soviet Union was in the form of trade and industrial ties. Despite the reduction in political and military cooperation, the economic relationship had proceeded relatively smoothly with further trade agreements being signed in March 1934 and April 1935.[56] The partnership was based on the appreciation of the mutual advantages to be reaped in the form of German access to raw materials and foreign exchange and the Soviet requirement for industrial machinery and technical assistance. It was these links that the Soviet leadership sought to utilise in 1935 in order to repair relations with Berlin. In June, following negotiations in Berlin, Hjalmar Schacht, the German Minister for Economic Affairs, offered the Soviet Union an expanded programme of trade to be financed by German loans over a period of ten years. The Soviet representatives assumed that the programme would be the first step in the restoration of relations but, despite nine months of negotiation, the only sign of progress was a Trade and Payments Treaty signed in April 1936.[57]

In fact such a *rapprochement* was not possible given Hitler's determination to maintain an element, if not of outward hostility, certainly of distance in Soviet–German relations. The value of any such relationship had to be weighed against the hostility and suspicion it would have created in Eastern Europe and especially in Poland which was at the centre of the proposed German network of bilateral non-aggression pacts. Poland's acquiescence was necessary to secure Germany's eastern frontiers as Hitler turned his attention to Western Europe with the intention of remilitarising the Rhineland. In addition, a stance of outward hostility to communism was a central pillar in the Nazi propaganda campaign designed to elicit sympathy within the capitalist world and justify the German rearmament programme. Given that Germany was now openly rearming and no longer needed military and economic facilities within the Soviet Union, the advantages presented by a renewal of close ties with the Soviet Union appeared to be far outweighed by the drawbacks that such a relationship would have produced.[58]

In order to contain the growing German menace, the Soviet Union turned increasingly to the major powers with a clear interest in maintaining the European status quo. In this context, while not totally abandoning attempts to improve relations with Germany, Litvinov continued to urge the League of Nations to reinforce the measures being taken for the organisation of a system of collective security. In an address to the League Council on 17 April 1935, Litvinov soundly denounced the German decision to reintroduce military conscription: 'this constitutes an infringement of the Covenant itself, and consequently, a violation of undertakings towards all the other members of the League.'[59]

During Anthony Eden's visit to Moscow in March 1935, the Soviet Commissar for Foreign Affairs outlined his perception of the problems confronting the League:

> The overwhelming majority of States are at the present moment vitally interested in the preservation of peace. If there are a few exceptions, the danger spots are precisely located and clearly defined.
>
> In these circumstances every State should examine and is examining the need to take steps which depend on it for averting the common danger. From the fact that the Covenant of the League of Nations provides for cases in which an attack on one State may be regarded as an act of war against all the members of the League, it ought to follow on the principle of the wise English proverb that 'prevention is better than cure', that all States should consider themselves threatened when the danger of war threatens even only one State.[60]

The following twelve months were to witness two vigorous challenges to the credibility and authority of the League of Nations with the Italian invasion of Abyssinia in October 1935 and the German remilitarisation of the Rhineland in March 1936. In both instances the Soviet Union declared itself in the vanguard of those nations prepared to uphold the Covenant of the League of Nations. On 22 November 1935, in response to Italian protest at the Soviet Union's support for the application of sanctions against Italy by members of the League, Litvinov declared:

> As a state the Soviet Union has not the slightest interest in the Italo–Abyssinian conflict and its outcome.
>
> The Soviet Government does not doubt that from the moment when the fact of the violation of Article 12 was established, no

member of the League of Nations . . . was entitled to evade the obligations arising from Article 16.

> Any other conduct would have meant a rejection of the principles of the League of Nations, a rejection of the collective organisation of security, the encouragement of aggression in the future, and a denial of the possibility of displaying international solidarity in the cause of maintaining and consolidating peace.[61]

Furthermore, the Soviet Union joined Rumania in advocating the expansion of sanctions against Italy to include goods such as oil, coal, iron and steel designed severely to disrupt the Italian war effort.[62] Litvinov admitted, however, that these measures would be meaningless without the unequivocal support of Britain and France. In an address to the Assembly of the League of Nations the British Foreign Secretary, Sir Samuel Hoare, on 12 September 1935, suggested that such support would be forthcoming:

> In conformity with its precise and explicit obligations, the League stands and my country stands with it, for the collective maintenance of the Covenant in its entirety, and particularly for steady and collective resistance to all acts of unprovoked aggression.

In an earlier section of his speech, however, Hoare had expressed concern that Britain and France were being saddled with the responsibility for making sanctions work: 'If risks for peace are to be run, they must be run by all. The security of the many cannot be ensured solely by the efforts of the few, however powerful they may be.'[63] It was, therefore, apparent that Hoare feared that the outcome of the employment of economic sanctions against Mussolini would be a Mediterranean war conducted largely between Britain, France and Italy. The prospect of such a conflict generated deep concern in both London and Paris particularly as the British Admiralty doubted its ability adequately to defend British possessions in the Mediterranean.[64] In addition, it appeared foolish actively to disrupt relations with Italy at a time when Mussolini's support was needed to lure Hitler into a security agreement. From the outset, therefore, Britain and France were reluctant to allow the Abyssinian issue to exacerbate relations with Italy. While, therefore, they paid lip-service to the denunciations of the Italian invasion which emanated from Geneva, they were also prepared to acquiesce to many of the Italian claims against Abyssinia in order to defuse the issue. This attempt to combine conciliation with coercion was unlikely to succeed given Mussolini's determination to challenge the League. Once Mussolini had declared that he would view the imposition of an embargo on the provision of oil supplies to Italy as an act of war, the western powers hastily rejected the imposition of extensive economic sanctions against Italy. The only solution appeared to lie in negotiation and compromise but now that Mussolini was able to negotiate from a position of strength, the outcome could only be in the form of a capitulation to Italian demands.[65] The weakness of the Anglo–French bargaining position was indicated by the Hoare–Laval plan which effectively bypassed the proceedings at Geneva and surrendered most of Abyssinia to Italian domination. In attempting to defend the scheme before the House of Commons, on 19 December 1935, Sir Samuel Hoare declared:

> I was shocked at the thought that we could lead Ethiopia to believe that the League of Nations could do more than was in its power, and that, when all was said and done, we would be faced with a terrible disappointment on the day that Ethiopia was completely destroyed as an independent State.[66]

In a report to the Central Executive Committee on 10 January 1936, Molotov alluded to this apparent cynical betrayal of the League of Nations:

> The Soviet Union alone declared that it bases itself on the principle of the equality and independence of Abyssinia . . . and that it cannot support any action of the League or of individual capitalist States which aims at violating this independence and equality. This policy of the Soviet Union, which distinguishes it in principle from the other members of the League of Nations, is one of extraordinary international significance and one which will yet yield valuable fruit.[67]

While the League of Nations continued its fruitless debate of the Abyssinian issue, a further challenge was presented with the German remilitarisation of the Rhineland on 7 March 1936. This act represented a clear breach of the commitments outlined in the Treaties of Versailles and Locarno. In addition, it threatened to negate the military value of the network of alliances so carefully nurtured by France in Eastern Europe in the post-war era. Ulam noted:

> Given the military technology of the time or the currently held military dogmas, German remilitarisation of the area would make those guarantees of very little value. Germany could fortify her western frontier, and Poland or Czechoslovakia could be over run while France and Germany would settle down to prolonged positional warfare behind their fortifications.[68]

At a meeting of the Council of the League of Nations, called in

London on 17 March 1936, Litvinov spoke out strongly against any temptation to acquiesce and accept the German action:

> We cannot preserve the League of Nations founded on the sanctity of international treaties (including the Covenant of the League itself) if we turn a blind eye to breaches of those treaties or confine ourselves to verbal protests, and take no more effective measures in defence of international undertaking.[69]

After rejecting the validity of the German suggestion that the ratification of the Franco–Soviet pact violated the terms of the Treaty of Locarno and, therefore, freed Germany from its obligations under the Locarno agreement, Litvinov concluded:

> I declare in the name of my Government its readiness to take part in all measures which may be proposed to the Council of the League by the Locarno Powers and will be acceptable to the other Members of the Council.[70]

Once again it appeared that action by the League of Nations depended entirely upon the stance adopted by Britain and France. Throughout January and February of 1936 the French Foreign Ministry had predicted the staging of a German attempt to remilitarise the Rhineland.[71] The French Foreign Minister, Flandin, attempted to gauge the reaction of the British government and the French War Office to just such an event, and in reply to his probings the War Ministry conceded that the French army did not have contingency plans for a campaign to reoccupy the Rhineland. On 24 February Flandin minuted:

> It must be established that the letter from the Minister of War only refers to certain 'guarantee' measures . . . whose purpose would be to secure us against a further development of German initiative; it contains nothing about the initiatives which France would take to intimidate her enemy or to make the enemy retreat.[72]

General Gamelin later admitted that the French army was in no position to drive German forces out of the Rhineland without a general mobilisation and guarantees of immediate support from Belgium and Britain.[73]

Despite a great deal of bluster from the French government, therefore, it was apparent that military action against Germany was unlikely without full British support and cooperation in both the military and diplomatic spheres. Militarily it seemed that Britain was as unprepared as France to mount any form of major European offensive. A military expeditionary force could not be organised for some time, and supremacy in the air and on the sea was far from certain. As N. H. Gibbs noted, the report of the Joint Planning Staff to the Chiefs of Staff on the condition of the armed forces in March 1936 concluded:

> For war with Germany with our present dispositions we were 'perilously exposed' in the air and 'completely open' to attack by sea. Air forces in general were considered 'utterly inadequate' for war with Germany at her present strength.[74]

Yet these factors were largely immaterial for, from the outset, the British government dismissed the possibility of war. The British Foreign Secretary, Anthony Eden, later claimed that Stanley Baldwin had established the parameters of action by instructing him that 'there would be no support in Britain for any military action by the French'.[75]

The limited nature of the British response to the German action was confirmed by the Foreign Secretary in the House of Commons on 9 March 1936. Eden argued that there was 'no reason to suppose that the present German action implied a threat of hostilities'.[76] The Foreign Secretary drew a clear distinction between remilitarisation of the Rhineland and invasion of French territory. In his interpretation, only the latter would constitute a flagrant infringement of the Locarno Treaty entitling France to respond militarily and expect British support.[77] This low-key approach was reflected in the military discussions convened between the British and French General Staffs on 15-16 April. Negotiations were restricted to an appreciation of the logistics of despatching two divisions to France 15 days after the commencement of hostilities rather than any attempt to produce a coordinated plan of campaign.[78]

Taking its lead from London the French reaction to the German remilitarisation of the Rhineland was based on the belief that the crisis presented an opportunity to move away from the outdated concepts of Locarno and Versailles and draw Germany into a new European security agreement. Attention, therefore, was focused not so much on Germany's disregard for its treaty obligations but rather towards moulding and expanding the German counter-proposals into a formula that could be utilised to rebuild the format of European security. In an address to the Council of the League of Nations on 17 March Litvinov denounced the Anglo–French stance and alluded to the danger of assuming that Germany would respect future treaty commitments if allowed to abrogate its existing obligations. Quoting from *Mein Kampf,* Litvinov continued:

> The political testament to the German nation for its external activity will, and must always, proclaim: Never permit two continental powers to arise in Europe. In every attempt to organise a second military power on the German frontier . . . you

> must see an attack on Germany, and you must consider it not only right, but your duty, to prevent such a State coming into existence by all possible means, including the use of force of arms, and if such a State has already come into being, it must once again be shattered.[79]

Litvinov claimed that the remilitarisation of the Rhineland was just one section of the overall scheme dedicated to 'setting up the hegemony of Germany over the whole European continent'.[80] In this light he argued that the network of non-aggression pacts advocated by Germany was designed to destabilise European security rather than contribute towards the establishment of an improved formula:

> This proposal of Mr Hitler's gives me the impression that we are faced with a new attempt to divide Europe into two or more parts, with the object of guaranteeing non-aggression for one part of Europe in order to acquire a free hand for dealing with other parts.
>
> . . . such a system of pacts can only increase the security of the aggressor and not the security of peace loving nations.[81]

On these grounds he stated that the League of Nations could not stand aside and allow Germany to break international agreements with impunity and, if necessary, the full weight of the League of Nations should be brought to bear against Germany. His words, however, were to no avail, for while the British government continued to pay lip-service to the principles enshrined in the Covenant of the League, in practice, it adhered firmly to the course of action outlined by Anthony Eden, and approved by the Cabinet on 9 March. In a paper placed before the Cabinet, Eden declared:

> The myth is now exploded that Herr Hitler only repudiates treaties imposed on Germany by force. We must be prepared for him to repudiate any treaty even if freely negotiated (a) when it becomes inconvenient, and (b) when Germany is sufficiently strong and the circumstances are otherwise favourable for doing so.
>
> On the other hand, owing to Germany's growing material strength and power of mischief in Europe, it is in our interest to conclude with her as far-reaching and enduring a settlement as possible whilst Herr Hitler is in the mood to do so. But on entering upon this policy we must bear in mind that, whatever time-limits may be laid down in such a settlement, Herr Hitler's signature can only be considered as valid under the conditions specified above.[82]

Britain and France, therefore, limited their response to a symbolic denunciation of the German decision to ignore its treaty obligations and concentrated their efforts towards examining and building upon the peace proposals offered by Hitler.[83]

It appeared that once again the authority of the League of Nations had been undermined and severely impaired. When the Assembly of the League of Nations met on 1 July 1936 to consider a further humiliation with the lifting of the ineffectual sanctions policy against Italy, Litvinov voiced his disappointment:

> We have met here to complete a page in the history of the League of Nations, a page in the history of international life which it will be impossible for us to read without a feeling of bitterness. We have to liquidate a course of action which was begun in fulfilment of our obligations as Members of the League to guarantee the independence of one of our fellow-Members, but which was not carried to its conclusion. Each of us must feel his measure of responsibility and of blame, which is not identical for all, and which depends, not only on what each of us did in fact, but also on the measure of our readiness to support every common action required by the circumstances.[84]

As an indication of the general lack of faith in the League of Nations, Litvinov placed heavy emphasis on the need to reform the structure of the organisation with a precise definition of acts which constituted aggression and a firm commitment that, once an act of aggression had been identified, the imposition of economic and, if necessary, military sanctions would be obligatory on all members.[85]

It appeared that Litvinov had conceded that the failure of the League of Nations satisfactorily to resolve the Abyssinian and Rhineland crises represented a severe blow to the principle of collective security. In addition, the German reoccupation of the Rhineland had effectively nullified the military credibility of the Franco–Soviet pact.[86] It seemed that throughout the crises Britain and France had consistently sought to appease the aggressors rather than uphold the Covenant of the League of Nations. In this light, Litvinov argued that they had played a central role in undermining the League. The truth of the matter, however, was that the Soviet Union was no more ready to go to war over the Rhineland or Abyssinian issues than were Britain or France. Max Beloff concluded:

> Once inside the League, the Soviet Union acted as a loyal and even enthusiastic member, but it was obviously no more willing than any other power to risk vital national interests for the sake of demonstrating its devotion to League principles.[87]

Throughout this period the goal of Soviet foreign policy remained firmly fixed on the maintenance of the status quo in Eastern Europe. In this context, as Litvinov had tacitly admitted on 14 May 1936, European security was far more important than the integrity of an African nation:

> Ethiopia does not interest me; it is necessary to see whether it is possible to obtain adequate pledges from Italy with regard to her general policy in Europe; if these pledges are sufficiently well defined, it will be worth while to say no more about it.[88]

The significance of the Abyssinian and Rhineland crises, therefore, lay not so much in the workings of the machinery of the League of Nations but rather as an indication of the determination of Britain and France to act resolutely to contain the threat of the revisionist powers dedicated to overthrowing elements of the international status quo. It seemed that the lack of resolve displayed by the western allies represented a severe blow to Soviet designs to utilise the mantle of collective security to shield its European frontiers. Yet, as Litvinov noted, all was by no means lost:

> if we cannot as yet rise to such heights of international solidarity we ought to see that every continent, and Europe, if only as a beginning, should be covered with a network of regional pacts, by virtue of which individual groups of States would undertake to defend particular regions from the aggressor, and the fulfilment of these regional obligations would be considered equivalent to the fulfilment of obligations under the covenant and would have the full support of all Members of the League.[89]

It appeared that the crises had highlighted the areas of weakness within the League of Nations and presented an opportunity to reassess its policy towards sanctions and the maintenance of security. In particular, Litvinov emphasised the need to develop regional security agreements.[90] The Soviet Union was no more interested than Britain and France in fighting for the defence of African or Asian states, but recognised the contribution to Soviet security that could be made by a pact of mutual assistance sponsored by the League of Nations in Eastern Europe. The Rhineland occupation had, therefore, ironically assisted the Soviet government by highlighting the need for the reform of the League of Nations and, as Molotov pointed out on 19 March in an interview for *Le Temps,* it had illustrated the need for East European states to form an alliance to resist German expansionism.[91]

If, however, in this period the Soviet Union sought to further its ties with Geneva, Paris and London, the possibility of a bilateral agreement with Berlin was not excluded. It is interesting to note that at the height of the Rhineland crisis on 19 March Molotov declared:

> There is a tendency among certain sections of the Soviet public towards an attitude of thorough going irreconcilability to the present rulers of Germany. . . .
>
> But the chief tendency, and the one determining the Soviet Government's policy, thinks an improvement in Soviet–German relations possible.[92]

There was no indication, however, of a desire by Germany to restore relations. Indeed Hitler's constant references to the communist menace continued to exacerbate links between the two states.[93] For Hitler the need to 'contain' the threat posed by communism was an invaluable weapon in justifying German rearmament. Furthermore, the suggestion of Soviet designs on Eastern Europe[94] could be used both to browbeat the nations of Central Europe into accepting German domination and also as a possible pretext for military occupation of nations 'threatened' by communist penetration. The initial focus of German attention was Poland. On 14 August Joachim von Ribbentrop discussed with the Polish Under-Secretary for Foreign Affairs the need for cooperation between the two nations:

> Both Poland and Germany were faced with a serious danger arising from the fact that the Soviets had not renounced the conception of world revolution.
>
> Chancellor Hitler could not make any compromise in relation to Russia, because the slightest deviation from his own present policy must open the way for the reign of Bolshevism in Germany. Von Ribbentrop considered that Poland was menaced by the danger of Bolshevism equally with Germany, and that the only way of counteracting this danger was the prevention of the catastrophe by crushing at their roots even the smallest sign of communism.[95]

Scaremongering, however, was not sufficient to draw Poland into the German orbit. The Polish Foreign Minister, Colonel Beck, was determined to maintain an element of distance in Poland's relations with both Berlin and Moscow. Indeed, by the latter half of 1936 there were signs that Beck was becoming increasingly disillusioned with the results of the tentative *rapprochement* initiated by the Polish–German non-aggression pact of January 1934, and was looking to restore relations with Paris, which had the advantage of both countering German pressure and giving Poland influence with the nations of the Little Entente.[96] Except for the signing of a German–Lithuanian commercial treaty, on 5 August 1936, German attempts to conclude bilateral agreements with the East European states met with little success. In particular, the Czechoslovakian government rejected

German overtures for a pact of non-aggression in October and December of 1936,[97] and reaffirmed its intention to respect its existing alliances and commitments.[98] Germany was successful, however, in achieving a degree of economic leverage over Yugoslavia and Rumania. The removal of the Rumanian Foreign Minister, Titulescu, in August 1936, was a major blow to Soviet attempts to improve relations with Rumania and undermined the credibility of the Soviet–Czech pact of mutual assistance which was dependent on the goodwill of the nations separating the two countries if the Soviet Union was ever required to come to the defence of Czechoslovakia.[99] In an attempt to repair relations, the Czech Foreign Minister, in May 1937, declared that he had received assurances that Yugoslavia and Rumania continued to support Czech links with the Soviet Union:

> I am not revealing any secret when I say that this concurrence on the part of our two allies has been confirmed again and again on various occasions without reserve.
>
> The questions of the recognition of the Soviet Union and of the Czechoslovak–Soviet Pact have thus from the very outset been absolutely clear within the ranks of the Little Entente.[100]

Yet while the Czech Foreign Minister sought to restore support for his government's links with Moscow, it was evident that Hitler's Germany was increasingly casting its shadow over East European affairs.

Although the Soviet Union watched the development of German overtures in Eastern Europe with vigilance, a further area for concern was provided by the links being established between Rome and Berlin. The Austro–German agreement of 11 July 1936, whereby Germany agreed to abstain from interference in Austrian domestic affairs, had cleared the path for a general *rapprochement* between the two nations.[101] While previously Hitler had been the primary exponent of anti-communist propaganda, Mussolini now began to speak of the need to oppose the communist menace. A further twist to the establishment of a broad anti-communist front was provided on 25 November 1936, by the signing of the Anti-Comintern pact between Japan and Germany. Following the conclusion of the agreement von Ribbentrop declared:

> Today a strong line of defence has been formed by two nations who are equally determined to bring to destruction every attempt at intervention in their two countries by the Communist International. Japan will never permit any dissemination of Bolshevism in the Far East. Germany is creating a bulwark against this pestilence in Central Europe. Finally Italy, as the Duce informs the world, will hoist the anti-Bolshevist barrier in the south.[102]

The anti-Soviet tenor of the agreement was inescapable. Von Ribbentrop later conceded: 'Naturally the Anti-Comintern Pact was partly political and directed against Russia, since Moscow was the driving force of the Comintern conception.'[103]

Although the Anti-Comintern pact was overtly restricted to the coordination of measures to prevent the expansion of communist influence, the Soviet Union could not ignore the possible military implications of an alliance between Germany and Japan. At Nuremberg, in September 1936, Hitler had spoken of the German need to control large tracts of the Soviet Union:

> If we had at our disposal the incalculable wealth and stores of raw materials of the Ural mountains and the unending fertile plains of the Ukraine to be exploited under National Socialist leadership, then we would produce, and our German people would swim, in plenty.[104]

In addition the pendulum of power in Japan appeared to be swinging away from the forces of moderation, following the successful military coup of February 1936. In March 1936 a Soviet–Mongolian pact of mutual assistance was concluded as a direct warning to Japan that the Soviet Union would not permit Japanese infiltration of the Mongolian People's Republic.[105] It appeared that the possible orchestration of German and Japanese policy towards the Soviet Union presented a major threat to Soviet security. At the Eighth Soviet Congress, on 28 November 1936, Litvinov declared his suspicion that the Anti-Comintern pact was accompanied by a secret military agreement between Japan, Italy and Germany directed not only against the Soviet Union but the whole concept of international security:

> The aggressive character of the recently concluded agreements follows if only from the fact that the participants are three States which withdrew from the League of Nations.
>
> All the three states, well known for their aggressiveness and their attempts against the territories of others, are fighting against the principles of collective security and the indivisibility of peace. This in itself lends a sinister character to these agreements and indicates their menace to universal peace, security and the interest of many countries.[106]

In response to this threat, Litvinov declared that the Soviet Union would redouble its efforts to ensure its security. Steps in this direction had in fact been taken in July and August of 1935 when the Seventh Congress of the Comintern had sought to create a united international socialist response to the threat perceived from fascism. In announcing the intention to forge a United Front, the General Secretary of the

Comintern, Georgi Dimitrov, outlined the task facing the organisation:

> How can fascism be prevented from coming to power and can fascism be overthrown after being victorious . . .?
>
> The just thing that must be done is to form a united front, to establish unity of action of the workers in every factory in every district, in every region, in every country, all over the world.[107]

This decision indicated an abandonment of the argument that fascism and social democracy were kindred spirits which demanded that communists break their ties with other socialist groups.[108] The United Front now urged communists to unite with their former rivals to form the nucleus of a popular movement drawing on all elements of the political spectrum prepared to combat fascism.[109] These tactics enjoyed a fair degree of success with the electoral victories of Popular Front governments in Spain and France during the course of 1936. However, beneath the promotion of an international response to fascism lay the determination to use whatever weapons that were at Moscow's disposal to ensure the security of the Soviet state. As Franz Borkenau noted, the United Front

> implied a wholesale overthrow of the basic principles of communism. Instead of the class struggle, co-operation with the bourgeoisie. Instead of the Soviet system, eulogy of democracy. Instead of internationalism, nationalism.[110]

The manipulation of the Comintern to serve the goals of Soviet foreign policy was indicated by the differing tactics adopted in France and the Far East. In Europe where there was no immediate military threat to Soviet territorial integrity the goal was primarily the containment of fascism rather than its destruction. The basis of the United Front in France was established in May 1935 when Stalin endorsed the French rearmament programme.[111] As a result of this decision the French Communist Party toned down its previous criticism of the rearmament programme and sought to establish links with the trade union movement and other socialist groups in a coalition against fascism. It was apparent, however, that as long as the fascist movement was restrained, the French Communist movement had no intention of surrendering its independence, and indeed continued its campaign to capture the leadership of the trade union organisation and oust its socialist rivals.[112] It was this ambivalent approach to the formation of the United Front that led Ulam to note:

> The conclusion is inescapable then, that the original aim of the Popular Front tactics, in so far as the Soviet leadership was concerned was defensive in nature. It was not to provide the

> Western countries with the resolution and the material means to fight Hitler. It was to make sure that they would not fall prey to fascism themselves and/or become allies of Hitler in a bloc against the USSR.[113]

While Stalin may have remained optimistic as to the ability of the western democracies to resist the ideological challenge of fascism and contain the growing military threat presented by Germany, cause for concern was generated by Japanese ambitions in China, Manchuria and Mongolia. The Soviet leadership suspected that if the Japanese army were successful in gaining control of most of China, it would then seek to move against the Soviet Far Eastern provinces. In response to this challenge while, in Europe, the communist movement continued to maintain a degree of independence in its dealings with its new left-wing allies, in China the Communist Party was instructed to seek a close alliance with its main rival the Kuomintang. The battle for the control of the resulting coalition was tacitly abandoned in favour of bolstering Chinese military opposition to the ambitions of the Japanese army. The basis of a working relationship between the Kuomintang and the communists was established in the spring of 1937 and followed in August 1937 by a Sino–Soviet pact of non-aggression.[114] The agreement effectively prevented China from adhering to the Anti-Comintern pact, and signified an improvement in Sino–Soviet relations which led to the provision of Soviet economic and military aid to China. The rationale behind this policy clearly evolved from the conclusion that if the Sino–Japanese conflict could be drawn out, the possibility of a Japanese assault on the Soviet Union's vulnerable eastern frontiers would be proportionately reduced. The difference between the Comintern tactics employed in Europe and the Far East succinctly indicated that Soviet security was placed before the promotion of international communism. In November 1937 Dimitrov conceded that the establishment of whether a body was to be classified as anti-Marxist rested basically upon its attitude towards the Soviet Union:

> The *historical dividing line* between the forces of Fascism, war and Capitalism on the one hand and the forces of peace, democracy and Socialism on the other hand is in fact becoming the *attitude* towards the Soviet Union.[115]

The decision to encourage European communists to take the offensive against fascism did, however, present several problems for the Soviet regime, particularly in relation to the civil war in Spain. While outwardly committed to assisting the Republican government against the Nationalist insurgents, it soon became apparent that, despite the formation of the International Brigades, and the provision of extensive military assistance, the Nationalist forces were slowly but steadily gaining the upper hand.[116] Although victory for Franco would represent a success for Italy and Germany, the Soviet Union was inhibited from mobilising further support for the Republicans by the desire not to impair its relations with Britain and France. Once Britain and France had opted for a policy of non-intervention it was feared that the spectacle of the Red Army operating in Spain would once again resurrect the spectre of communism aggressively seeking to expand its international influence. The Soviet Union, therefore, sought repeatedly to emphasise that the Republican government was not communist, but a broad coalition of the parties of the political left.[117] In addition, on a military level, given the absence of positive support from Britain and France, it was dubious as to whether Soviet military intervention could engineer a Republican victory. As a matter of prestige Mussolini and, to a lesser extent, Hitler were committed to sponsoring a Nationalist victory in Spain. Intervention, therefore, threatened to draw the Soviet Union deeper into a European war that was not of strategic importance to Soviet security. In this light, despite the commitment to oppose fascism, Soviet support for the Republican army did not attempt to match the flow of men and material from Germany and Italy, and indeed Stalin was forced to the conclusion that wider considerations might be best served by an end to the conflict with a Nationalist victory.

In this light, the development of the Popular Front was primarily designed to contain the threat of fascism while reassuring the western democracies that communism was no longer an international menace. Yet while Stalin repeatedly emphasised that the Soviet Union did not seek to promote international revolution, he failed to overcome the barriers of mistrust and suspicion which had traditionally clouded relations between the Soviet Union and the western powers.[118] It appeared that Britain and France viewed the promotion of left-wing coalitions between trade unions and political activists with increasing trepidation. Certainly the strikes and demonstrations which followed the installation of the Popular Front government in France generated increasing alarm and suspicion.[119] Isaac Deutscher noted:

> Thus by a curious dialectical process the Popular Fronts defeated their own purposes. They had set out to reconcile the bourgeois West with Russia; they increased the estrangement.[120]

As the Soviet Union entered the third year of membership of the League of Nations the forces of fascism appeared to be gathering momentum while the League looked on helplessly from the sidelines. On 28 November 1936, in an address to the Eighth Soviet Congress, Litvinov declared:

> Fascism carries out its preparations for the achievement of its aggressive aims not only by increasing its armaments at an incredible rate, but also by releasing itself unilaterally from all international obligations or simply violating them when this suits it; by avoiding all international cooperation for the strengthening of peace; by attempting to undermine the international organisations which are called upon to protect peace; by waging a campaign for disuniting other countries and preventing the collective organisation of security.[121]

> Fascism directs its fiery arrows particularly against the Soviet state, ostensibly because the ideas of communism are professed there, but in reality because it is the object of the predatory appetites of fascism, and also an obstacle to its aims of conquest in other directions.[122]

The Commissar for Foreign Affairs referred in particular to the abject failure of the League of Nations to meet the challenges presented by the Abyssinian and Rhineland crises. He argued, furthermore, that the Anti-Comintern pact was a façade used by Germany, Italy and Japan to conceal ambitions based 'on contempt for peace, on principles of aggression and plunder, and which are on the lookout for opportunities of grabbing everything which is unprotected'.[123] Further force was added to Litvinov's words by the course of events in Spain and China in the following twelve months which served to confirm the conclusion that the League of Nations was largely ineffectual. On 27 November 1937, Litvinov once again chronicled the failures of the organisation as German and Italian troops poured into Spain:

> As a result the internal Spanish conflict, which the Spanish Government could have settled in a few weeks, grows into a huge armed conflict which has lasted now for more than a year and to which no end is yet in sight.[124]

> Take another example — the Far East. Japan is flooding China with her troops, occupying one province after another, shelling and bombing Chinese towns — in short, is doing everything that used to be called 'war'.[125]

Litvinov focused on the inability of the League of Nations to act decisively:

> China applies to the League of Nations for protection referring to the corresponding points in the League Covenant. The League forms a committee, the committee appoints a sub-committee, and the latter elects an editorial committee. A paper is drafted and addressed to Japan: 'We do not approve of your offensive.

> Probably it is based on a misunderstanding. Please come to confirm this, and, lest you feel lonely among us, we have invited your kindred spirit and friend Germany.' From Japan comes confirmation that there is no misunderstanding at all, that she is on the warpath quite deliberately and agrees to discuss matters only with China and only on terms of the latter's surrender.[126]

In assessing the League's record, the Soviet Commissar declared that the irresolution and shortsightedness of Britain and France had played a significant role in undermining the League's credibility. Litvinov concluded that Britain and France had failed to comprehend the threat presented by the fascist powers:

> I see it as a puzzle to you how experienced bourgeois diplomats could fail to understand the meaning of the aggressor's tactics. You think they are only pretending to disbelieve the aggressor's statements and, under cover of negotiations for confirmation and explanations, they are grouping for a deal with the aggressor. You can think so if you like, but my position does not allow me to express such doubts, and I must leave them to your responsibility.[127]

As an indication of growing disillusionment with the League of Nations, Litvinov emphasised that, although it would continue to foster the cause of collective security, the Soviet Union could not look solely on the League of Nations to ensure its territorial integrity, and must rely on its own military forces to secure its frontiers from attack.[128] The same point had also been made by Maisky, the Soviet Ambassador to London, in March 1937:

> the strategic position of the USSR which represents a great Continental bloc stretching from the Baltic to the Pacific is very strong and, in any case, less vulnerable than the position of some other countries. We have only two frontiers — in the west and in the far east — to defend, and I betray no military secret when I say that these two frontiers during the last few years have been made well nigh impregnable by the great fortifications, by the large armies well equipped with all modern appliances, and by the huge air force.[129]

This determination to stress the strength and independence of the Soviet state indicated that, despite membership of the League, Soviet foreign policy still followed the declaration made by Stalin at the Seventeenth Congress of the CPSU on 26 January 1934:

> Our orientation in the past and our orientation at the present time is toward the USSR, and toward the USSR alone. And if the

> interests of the USSR demand rapprochement with one country or another which is not interested in disturbing peace, we take this step without hesitation.[130]

Soviet interests in 1937, therefore, as in 1934, lay primarily in securing Soviet territorial integrity. It was the challenge presented by Japanese expansionism in the Far East and German ambitions in Eastern Europe which drove the Soviet Union to search for an understanding with the revisionist powers, and, when this proved largely fruitless, to move increasingly towards an alliance with Britain and France.[131]

Despite membership of the League of Nations, Soviet interests were still dictated by regional defensive considerations.[132] The Soviet Union was only interested in Abyssinia, Manchuria, Spain, the Rhineland and China in so far as they represented issues that could be manipulated to forge a coalition of nations to oppose German ambitions in Eastern Europe and Japanese expansionism in the Far East. When the western democracies showed more inclination to conciliate the fascist powers than oppose them, Soviet interest in the League of Nations declined proportionately. In this context the threatened withdrawal of the Soviet Union from Geneva did not represent a radical reorientation of Soviet strategy in the sense that an isolationist mentality had continually pervaded Soviet attitudes to foreign affairs with the belief that the ideological gulf between socialism and capitalism effectively precluded any real understanding between the Soviet Union and the outside world.[133] The Soviet *rapprochement* with France and Britain was never likely to overcome the barriers of mistrust and suspicion erected and maintained by both sides and was no more than a strategic manoeuvre in the wider game of international diplomacy. The almost mercenary nature of Soviet foreign policy was hinted at by Litvinov on 28 November 1936:

> The Soviet Union, however, does not beg to be invited to any unions, any blocs, any combinations. She will calmly let other States weigh and evaluate the advantages which can be derived for peace from close co-operation with the Soviet Union and understand that the Soviet Union can give more than receive.[134]

That the Soviet Union, by 1937, should begin to turn away from *rapprochement* with Britain and France was indicative of the latters' failure to serve Soviet interests by restraining Germany and Japan. Arnold J. Toynbee concluded of Anglo–French policy in this period:

> They made their momentous choice neither on the absolute criterion of morality nor on the relative criterion of expediency but on that trivial distinction between this moment and the next,

which keeps the sluggard cowering between the blankets when the house is burning over his head.[135]

Yet the Soviet Union was as guilty as Britain and France in undermining the credibility of collective security for its staunchly defensive posture also demanded conciliation rather than confrontation in spheres not of immediate strategic importance to Soviet interests. Although the remaining links with Britain and France were valuable in preventing the expansion of the anti-Comintern front and also in presenting the Soviet Union with an aura of international respectability, by 1937 the darkening international horizon demanded that the Soviet Union reassess its foreign strategy. The inherent adaptability of Soviet foreign policy had been noted by Count Werner von Schulenberg, the German Ambassador to Moscow:

> If the Soviet Union has sided with the democracies and the League of Nations during the last few years it has done so because Germany aims not merely at the restoration of her pre-war boundaries and the rights denied her by Versailles, but also pursues an open and 'mad' anti-Soviet policy and a policy of unlimited aggression.[136]
>
> Litvinov indicates that Soviet policy whose aim it was only a few years ago to collaborate as closely as possible with the democratic great powers and to be admitted to the circles of these states itself will henceforth — without abandoning the principle of collective security — break with the policy of the western powers and decide in each case whether its own interests require cooperation with England and France.[137]

Notes

1. Jane Degras (ed.), *Soviet Documents on Foreign Policy*. Vol. 3: *1933–1941* (New York, 1978), Litvinov's speech at the League Assembly on the entry of the USSR into the League of Nations, Geneva, 18 September 1934, pp. 90-1.
2. Ibid., p. 94.
3. Ibid., p. 96.
4. Ibid.
5. Ibid., Extracts from a speech by Litvinov on foreign affairs to the Central Executive Committee, 29 December 1933, pp. 48-61.
6. Ibid., p. 55.
7. Ibid., p. 57.
8. Ibid., p. 59.
9. Ibid., p. 51.

10. Ibid., Extracts from an interview between Stalin and Duranty of the *New York Times,* on the Soviet attitude to the League of Nations, 25 December 1933, p. 45.
11. Max Beloff, *The Foreign Policy of Soviet Russia.* Vol. I: *1929–1936* (London, 1947), pp. 198-9.
12. Degras, Litvinov's speech at the League Assembly on the entry of the USSR into the League of Nations, Geneva, 18 September 1934, pp. 95-6.
13. Ibid., Extracts from Molotov's report to the Seventh Soviet Congress, 25 January 1935, pp. 95-6.
14. Ibid., pp. 103-7.
15. Paul Haynes, *The Twentieth Century* (London, 1978), pp. 251-8.
16. Sir John Simon, *Retrospect* (London, 1952), p. 195.
17. Arnold Wolfers, *Britain and France between Two Wars* (New York, 1966), p. 274.
18. Ibid., pp. 274-5.
19. Sir Charles Petrie, *The Life and Letters of the Rt Hon. Sir Austen Chamberlain,* Vol. II (London, 1940), p. 258.
20. Louis Fischer, *Russia's Road from Peace to War* (New York, 1969), pp. 249-50.
21. Ibid., p. 268.
22. Simon, p. 200.
23. Ibid.
24. Anthony Eden, *The Eden Memoirs.* Vol. I: *Facing the Dictators* (London, 1962), p. 135.
25. Simon, p. 203.
26. Eden, pp. 135-41.
27. Ibid.
28. Simon, p. 203.
29. Wolfers, p. 278.
30. Degras, Speech by Litvinov at a reception to the French Foreign Minister, Laval, 13 May 1935, pp. 130-1.
31. *Documents on German Foreign Policy, 1919–39,* Series C, Vol. 2, State Secretary Bulow to Ambassador Nadolny, 12 February 1934, pp. 474-7.
32. Ibid., Vol. 4, Ambassador in Moscow to Foreign Ministry, p. 129.
33. Adam B. Ulam, *Expansion and Coexistence, The History of Soviet Foreign Policy, 1917–67* (London, 1968), pp. 223-4.
34. Beloff, pp. 152-4.
35. J. Nere, *The Foreign Policy of France from 1914 to 1945* (London, 1975), pp. 170-1.
36. Wolfers, p. 141.
37. Ibid.
38. Ibid., p. 310.
39. Fischer, p. 264.
40. Nere, p. 164.
41. Ibid., p. 171.
42. Wolfers, pp. 139-41.

43. Gerhard L. Weinberg, *The Foreign Policy of Hitler's Germany: Diplomatic Revolution in Europe: 1933–36* (London, 1970), p. 219.
44. Degras, Reply to the Anglo–French communiqué on the London negotiations on proposals for a European settlement, 20 February 1935, p. 119.
45. Eden, p. 155.
46. Ulam, p. 225.
47. Weinberg, pp. 74-81.
48. Beloff, p. 155.
49. Weinberg, p. 75.
50. Deutscher, pp. 400-6.
51. Weinberg, pp. 74-81.
52. *DGFP,* Series C, Vol. 1, Memorandum by the State Secretary, Berlin, 26 September 1933, pp. 851-3.
53. Degras, Extracts from a report by Stalin to the Seventeenth Congress of the CPSU, 26 January 1934, pp. 70-1.
54. Weinberg, pp. 181-5.
55. Ibid., p. 220.
56. Beloff, p. 55.
57. Weinberg, pp. 219-24.
58. Ibid.
59. Degras, Speech by Litvinov at the League Council on German violation of the Versailles Treaty, 17 April 1935, pp. 127-9.
60. Ibid., Speech by Litvinov at a reception to Mr Eden during his visit to Moscow, 28 March 1935, pp. 122-4.
61. Ibid., Reply to the Italian note: addressed to the states represented on the League of Nations Coordination Committee: Note from Litvinov to the Italian Ambassador in Moscow, 22 November 1935, pp. 149-50.
62. Beloff, p. 203.
63. Viscount Templewood, *Nine Troubled Years* (London, 1954), p. 170.
64. Wolfers, pp. 358-63.
65. Ibid.
66. Parliamentary Debates, House of Commons, 19 December 1935, Vol. 307, Cols 2007-2017.
67. Degras, Extracts from a report by Molotov to the Central Executive Committee, 10 January 1936, pp. 151-8.
68. Ulam, p. 234.
69. Degras, Statement by Litvinov at the Council of the League of Nations on the remilitarisation of the Rhineland, 17 March 1936, pp. 170-8.
70. Ibid., p. 178.
71. Nere, pp. 184-6.
72. Ibid., p. 187.
73. Ibid., pp. 187-8; see also pp. 333-5.
74. N. H. Gibbs, *Grand Strategy*. Vol. I: *Rearmament Policy* (London, 1976), pp. 246-9.
75. Eden, p. 343.
76. Parliamentary Debates, House of Commons, 9 March 1936, Vol. 390, Col. 1812.

77. Wolfers, pp. 45-58.
78. Nere, p. 197.
79. Degras, Statement by Litvinov at the Council of the League of Nations on the remilitarisation of the Rhineland, 17 March 1936, pp. 170-8.
80. Ibid., pp. 173-4.
81. Ibid., pp. 175-6.
82. Eden, p. 345.
83. Ibid., pp. 360-7.
84. Degras, Extracts from a statement by Litvinov at the League of Nations Assembly on the Italo–Abyssinian dispute, 1 July 1936, pp. 194-9.
85. Ibid.
86. Ulam, p. 234.
87. Beloff, p. 137.
88. Nere, p. 193.
89. Degras, Extracts from a statement by Litvinov at the League of Nations Assembly on the Italo–Abyssinian dispute, 1 July 1936, p. 199.
90. Ibid., pp. 197-9.
91. Degras, Extracts from an interview given by Molotov to M. Chastenet of *Le Temps,* on the reoccupation of the Rhineland and Soviet foreign policy, 19 March 1936, pp. 182-5.
92. Ibid.
93. Weinberg, pp. 310-12.
94. Max Beloff, *The Foreign Policy of Soviet Russia, 1929–1941*. Vol. II: *1936–1941* (London, 1949), pp. 68-9.
95. Ibid., p. 58.
96. Ibid., p. 74.
97. Ibid., p. 78.
98. Ibid., p. 69.
99. Ibid., pp. 71-2.
100. Ibid., pp. 73-4.
101. Weinberg, pp. 264-71.
102. Beloff, Vol. II, p. 63.
103. Joachim von Ribbentrop, *The Ribbentrop Memoirs* (London, 1954), p. 76.
104. Beloff, Vol. II, p. 58.
105. Frederick L. Schuman, *Soviet Politics* (London, 1948), p. 251.
106. Degras, Extracts from Litvinov's speech at the Eighth Soviet Congress, 28 November 1936, pp. 224-5.
107. Richard F. Rosser, *Soviet Foreign Policy* (New Jersey, 1969), p. 165.
108. Deutscher, pp. 411-12.
109. Beloff, Vol. II, pp. 16-17.
110. Franz Borkenau, *World Communism,* p. 387. Quoted in Rosser, p. 165.
111. Degras, Communiqué on the visit of M. Laval, French Foreign Minister, to Moscow, 16 May 1935, pp. 131-2.
112. Beloff, Vol. II, p. 17.

113. Ulam, p. 229.
114. Beloff, Vol. II, pp. 181-2.
115. Ibid., pp. 20-1.
116. Ibid., pp. 28-38.
117. Isaac Deutscher, *Stalin: A Political Biography* (London, 1966), pp. 415-17.
118. Deutscher, pp. 413-15.
119. Charles A. Micaud, *The French Right and Nazi Germany 1933–1939, A Study of Public Opinion* (New York, 1972), pp. 12-23.
120. Deutscher, p. 414.
121. Degras, Extracts from Litvinov's speech at the Eighth Soviet Congress, 28 November 1936, pp. 220-6.
122. Ibid., p. 222.
123. Ibid., p. 226.
124. Degras, Extracts from an election speech by Litvinov on the international situation, 27 November 1937, pp. 266-8.
125. Ibid.
126. Ibid.
127. Ibid., p. 268.
128. Ibid.
129. Degras, Extracts from a speech by the Soviet Ambassador in London on the war danger, 13 March 1937, pp. 236-8.
130. Degras, Extracts from a report by Stalin to the Seventeenth Congress of the CPSU, 26 January 1934, p. 70.
131. A. R. Peters, R. H. Haigh and D. S. Morris, 'In Search of Peace', Sheffield City Polytechnic, Department of Public Sector Administration, Occasional Paper, pp. 29-47.
132. Henry L. Roberts, *Maxim Litvinov,* in Gordon A. Craig and Felix Gilbert, *The Diplomats 1919–39.* Vol. 2: *The Thirties* (New York, 1977), p. 364.
133. Ibid.
134. Degras, Extracts from Litvinov's speech at the Eighth Congress, 28 November 1936, pp. 220-6.
135. Arnold J. Toynbee, quoted in Schuman, p. 279.
136. *DGFP,* Series D, Vol. 1, Ambassador in Soviet Union to Foreign Ministry, 23 June 1938, pp. 928-9.
137. Ibid.

3 A Question of Balance

On 27 November 1937, in a speech delivered in Leningrad, the Soviet Commissar for Foreign Affairs, Maxim Litvinov, surveyed the course of international relations during the three years that had elapsed since the Soviet Union's accession to the League of Nations in September 1934. Litvinov made no attempt to disguise his conviction that the pillars supporting the international status quo were being progressively eroded.[1] The Soviet Commissar referred specifically to those elements which sought to undermine the fragile foundations of collective security and international law:

> there are three States which without any embarrassment, publicly, vociferously, day after day, announce their determination to disregard all international laws . . . even those they are signatory to, their determination to seize other people's territories wherever they get the chance, and for that reason reject any collective collaboration in the organisation of peace. They declare this aggressive policy of theirs as plain as can be, even with the utmost cynicism, and not only declare it, but are actually putting it into practice in some places.[2]

In addition to this assault on the policies being pursued by Germany, Italy and Japan, Litvinov was equally scathing in his criticism of the members of the international community that had refused fully to acknowledge the aggressive intentions of the revisionist states, and had failed to fulfil their obligation to uphold the Covenant of the League of Nations and the façade of collective security. The Soviet

Commissar roundly condemned and mocked their naive and short-sighted attitude:

> All these States seem to recognise that there is a grave danger emanating from several fascist and aggressive States, threatening peace and their own interests. They accept in principle the idea of collective security upon which the League of Nations was founded, but they go no further than words and declarations, and words and declarations cut no ice with the aggressor.[3]

In addition, Litvinov denounced the machinations at Geneva which produced innumerable committees of inquiry all seeking to obscure the challenge presented by the aggressors and evade the obligation to uphold international agreements:

> The aggressive countries are gaining new positions for further aggression, and the feeling that international law can be broken with impunity and that the so-called Great Powers are helpless, gives rise to new acts of aggression in other parts of the world.[4]

It appeared that the Soviet Union's attempts to foster the cause of collective security had received scant support from Britain and France:

> As we are concerned that peace be maintained not only near our frontiers, but that the security of all peoples be ensured, and as we act on the principle that peace is indivisible, we have agreed to take part in regional pacts of mutual assistance, we have concluded such pacts with France and Czechoslovakia, we have joined the League of Nations to test it as an instrument of peace, we take part in all international conferences and conventions called towards the better organisation of peace and collective security. Unfortunately, not all States, not even all leading States, display the same sincerity, the same consistency, and the same readiness to carry out existing or sometimes even projected measures for the organisation of peace as the Soviet Government.[5]

Litvinov's speech represented a direct attack on the 'bourgeois' diplomacy of the western powers which instead of opposing aggression sought to accommodate the demands of the revisionist nations. Given the venom with which he launched his assault it might have been construed that the Soviet Union was about to turn its back on the League of Nations.[6] In the latter half of his speech, however, the Soviet Commissar outlined his belief that the solution to the problem lay not in dismantling the League but rather in refining its machinery.[7] He, therefore, turned once again to the subject of reform and particularly to the problem of establishing a commitment to universal values and guidelines for international conduct.[8] The difficulties inherent within such an approach, he argued, had continually undermined the credibility of the proceedings at Geneva.[9] Looking at the League's record, the Soviet Commissar declared:

> I recommend these results to the attention of the advocates of universality. Let them meditate on the causes of these results, and they will realise that it is illusory to hope for successful co-operation between States which pursue different ends, which have opposite conceptions of international life and of the mutual rights and duties of people.
>
> Between aggression and non-aggression, between peace and war, there can be no synthesis.[10]

Therefore, while outlining his determination to reinforce rather than abandon Geneva, Litvinov indicated the need to reorient attitudes towards acceptance that negotiations with the revisionist powers were of little value unless backed by the threat of economic and military sanctions. In this context the Soviet Commissar sought to steer the League towards the establishment of purely regional pacts of assistance where nations would have a positive stake in acting to deter aggression. This policy was supported by persistent warnings to Britain, France and the United States of America of the penalties that would result from a failure to contain Italian, German and Japanese expansionism. Joseph E. Davies, United States Ambassador to the Soviet Union, noted that in conversation with Litvinov, on 4 February 1937, the Soviet Commissar outlined his belief

> that Hitler's policy had not changed from that which he had announced in his book *Mein Kampf*; that he was dominated by a lust for conquest and for the domination of Europe; that he could not understand why Great Britain could not see that once Hitler dominated Europe he would swallow the British Isles also.[11]

In the following twelve months Litvinov repeatedly emphasised to Davies the danger of appeasing Hitler and the need to present a resolute front.[12] Of their discussion on 11 November 1937, Davies recorded:

> He said that the Soviet Union was already prepared to take a strong stand if it were in co-operation with France, England and the United States; and that the Soviet Union was really seriously interested in the cessation of hostilities and in the immediate establishment of collective security and peace.[13]

However, alongside these declarations of good faith, there was increasing evidence of Soviet impatience with the lack of resolution displayed by the western powers. While declaring its faith in the principle of collective security, the Soviet government emphasised that its military forces were in a position to defend Soviet territorial integrity with or without assistance from the League.[14] This implicit warning to the western powers was underlined by Stalin, on 12 February 1938, when he readopted the distinction between socialist and non-socialist nations as the basis for his analysis of international relations. In previous years the attacks launched on 'revisionism' had formed the basis of the Soviet Union's reason for an understanding with the League.[15] This reversion to Marxist orthodoxy was a clear indication of Moscow's disenchantment with the proceedings at Geneva.[16]

If, however, Soviet interest in the League was waning it was dubious as to whether the British and French governments were unduly concerned at the prospect of a deterioration of links with Moscow. Indeed, despite the conclusion of the Franco–Soviet pact,[17] the lack of attention given to the establishment of military planning to implement the pledges of mutual assistance suggested that successive French governments saw the relationship as of only secondary value in containing German ambitions, and continued to look to Britain as the central pillar in upholding the European status quo.[18] This scepticism as to the value of an alliance with the Soviet Union was certainly shared by the British government. Although Britain had formally recognised the Soviet regime in 1924, relations between the two nations had been continually hampered by mistrust and barely concealed hostility. It was not until 1935 that a British minister made a formal visit to Moscow[19] and, although Anthony Eden considered that his discussions with Stalin and Litvinov had made significant inroads in reducing Soviet mistrust of British intentions, he was the first to admit that many of his colleagues remained innately hostile to the widening of relations with a communist government:

> Two points of view were, however, strongly held in the Cabinet and between them they might militate against any effective pursuit of the openings the Moscow visit had created. Some, religious in their views, regarded communism as anti-Christ. Others were brave enough to consider supping with the devil, but doubted whether he had much fare to offer. There was an almost universal opinion in Britain that the military power of the Soviets was in disarray and of poor quality.
>
> These exaggerated estimates were damaging to Anglo–Russian relations up to the moment when German troops crossed the Soviet frontier.[20]

Fear of the communist spectre and of traditional Russian expansionist designs in Eastern Europe continually clouded Anglo–French relations with the Soviet Union and led the western powers to exclude the Soviet regime from deliberations on the future status of Europe.[21] Neville Chamberlain spoke for most of the European leaders when on 21 February 1938 he declared: 'the peace of Europe must depend on the attitude of the four major powers of Europe; Germany, Italy, France and ourselves'.[22]

Undoubtedly suspicion of the Soviet Union was reinforced by doubts as to the ability of the Red Army to make an effective contribution to the enforcement of collective security. The French Foreign Minister, Delbos, informed Chamberlain that the French General Staff rated the capability of Soviet military forces below that of even the Rumanian army[23] as a result of the purges conducted in the officer ranks.[24] As early as July 1937 Joseph E. Davies had expressed fears about the impact of the purges on the Red Army and the resulting reduction in international confidence in its effectiveness:

> It now looks as if the loyalty of the army to the Stalin government has not been weakened. If that is so, then the government will be stronger than ever internally because it has with characteristic speed killed off all potential leadership. The pity of it all is that in so doing he has destroyed the confidence of western Europe in the strength of his army, and in the strength of his government; that has also weakened the confidence of both England and France in the strength of the Russian army, and has weakened the democratic bloc in western Europe, and that is serious, for the only real hope for peace is a London–Paris–Moscow axis.[25]

Given the question marks placed against the Red Army and the fears aroused by Soviet intervention in the Spanish civil war, it was apparent that Britain and France were looking increasingly for a direct settlement of their differences with Germany.[26] In addition, as Hitler,[27] along with many of the East European nations,[28] had repeatedly stated his aversion to communism, it appeared that the western powers could gain little from a concerted effort to improve relations with Moscow.[29]

The Anglo–French decision to deal directly with Germany and Italy without reference to the Soviet Union was clearly discernible in the latter half of 1937. In essence, Chamberlain believed that both Hitler and Mussolini were acting upon rational criteria in the pursuit of limited goals and, therefore, grounds existed for a mutually acceptable settlement. Chamberlain outlined this conviction on 16 January 1938:

> in the absence of a powerful ally and until our armaments are completed, we must adjust our foreign policy to our circumstances and even bear with patience and good humour actions

> which we would like to treat in very different fashion. It is indeed the human side of the dictators that makes them dangerous, but on the other hand, it is the side on which they can be approached with the greatest hope of successful issue.
>
> I am about to enter upon a fresh attempt to reach a reasonable understanding with both Germany and Italy, and I am by no means unhopeful of getting results.[30]

This conviction was probably prompted by the negotiations undertaken by Lord Halifax with Hitler in November 1937.[31] During the course of wide-ranging discussions Hitler limited his demands to the protection of Germanic peoples in Czechoslovakia and Austria, and the establishment of a military force at a level consistent with the adequate defence of German frontiers.[32] Chamberlain later noted of the negotiations:

> Now here it seems to me is a fair basis of discussion, though no doubt all these points bristle with difficulties. But I don't see why we should not say to Germany, 'give us satisfactory assurances that you won't use force to deal with the Austrians and Czechoslovakians, and we will give you similar assurances that we won't use force to prevent the changes you want, if you can get them by peaceful means'.[33]

This theme was taken up by the British Ambassador to Berlin, Nevile Henderson, in a conversation with Hitler on 3 March 1938.[34] Hitler was obviously preoccupied with the future status of the German minorities within Austria and Czechoslovakia. Henderson repeated that the British government had no objection to territorial adjustments as long as they were carried out by peaceful means and added 'he . . . had often expressed himself in favour of the *Anschluss*.'[35] The Anglo–German discussions were paralleled by similar feelers for a settlement of Anglo–Italian differences including British recognition of Italian sovereignty in Abyssinia and the withdrawal of Italian 'volunteers' from Spain.[36] Such was Chamberlain's conviction that an agreement with Italy was attainable and also of vital importance in gaining Italian support for the restraint of German ambitions that he was prepared to risk an open division with his Foreign Secretary on the matter and eventually to see Eden replaced by the more pliable Halifax.[37] On 19 February 1938, at the height of the confrontation with Eden, Chamberlain emphasised the priority that he assigned to the pursuit of an agreement with Rome and warned of the danger of refusing the initiatives broadcast from Rome in January and February of 1938:

> the dictators would be driven closer together, the last strand of

> Austrian independence would be lost, the Balkan countries would feel compelled to turn towards their powerful neighbours, Czechoslovakia would be swallowed, France would either have to submit to German domination or fight, in which case we should almost certainly be drawn in.[38]

Naturally, Hitler and Mussolini were not slow to sense and exploit the apparent Anglo–French determination to pursue a negotiated agreement and sanction concessions in certain quarters in order to facilitate such an agreement. During the months of January and February of 1938 Hitler steadily increased the tempo of pressure exerted upon Austria and Czechoslovakia.[39] On 20 February 1938, Hitler declared that German interests included: 'the protection of those fellow Germans who live beyond our frontiers and are unable to ensure for themselves the right to a general freedom, personal, political and ideological.'[40] In addition, he alluded once again to the need to rearm in order to defend Eastern Europe from communist penetration. On 3 March 1938, in an interview with the British Ambassador, Henderson, Hitler warned:

> It was a matter of life and death to Germany to protect her position in central Europe, and she must arm against any attack by Soviet Russia, which naturally could never be checked by the Border States or by Poland.[41]

It was apparent that Hitler was intent on laying claim to Austria and Czechoslovakia as lying within the German sphere of interest. In the following twelve months, with the German occupation of Austria on 12 March 1938 and the conclusion of the Munich agreement on 30 September 1938, significant steps were taken to realise this goal. In both instances the Soviet Union both predicted the course of events and sought to mobilise international opinion to oppose the expansion of German influence. On 11 November 1937, Litvinov warned Joseph Davies that he was 'extremely pessimistic' as to the future integrity of Austria.[42] In addition, *Pravda* called for international action to defend Austrian independence against aggression as early as 28 September 1937.[43] The German military occupation of Austria followed by its incorporation within the German Reich two days later produced a storm of criticism in the Soviet press directed not only against what it termed blatant German 'aggression' but also Anglo–French vacillation which had allowed such an act to be perpetrated.[44] In an attempt to bolster opposition to German expansion, Litvinov reaffirmed Soviet treaty commitments to Czechoslovakia and, on 17 March 1938, launched a further tirade against the *Anschluss*:

> the Soviet Government has voiced a warning that international

> inaction and the impunity of aggression in one case would inexorably lead to the repetition and multiplication of similar cases.
>
> Unfortunately international developments have justified these warnings. They received new confirmation in the armed invasion of Austria and in the forcible deprivation of the Austrian people of their political, economic and cultural independence.[45]

Litvinov clearly identified Czechoslovakia as the nation now most menaced by Germany and advocated collective action to maintain Czechoslovakian independence:

> I can state on its [the Soviet Union's] behalf that on its part it is ready as before to participate in collective actions which would be decided upon jointly with it and which would aim at checking the further development of aggression and at eliminating the increased danger of a new world massacre.
>
> It is prepared immediately to take up in the League of Nations or outside of it the discussion with other powers of the practical measures which the circumstances demand. It may be too late tomorrow.[46]

The speech was followed by formal approaches to Britain, France and the United States to open negotiations to establish measures to contain any future acts of aggression.[47] Following Chamberlain's rejection of this proposal, on 24 March 1938,[48] Davies could only conclude that Anglo–French policy was playing into the hands of Germany and that this would increasingly drive a wedge between Britain and France, on the one hand, and the Soviet Union on the other.[49] As Litvinov predicted, having secured Austria, the focus of attention in Eastern Europe turned increasingly towards the German demand for the reunification of the Czechoslovakian Sudetenland with the German Reich.[50] The German campaign, which was carefully orchestrated by von Ribbentrop at various meetings with the German Sudeten leaders, began to gather momentum in the spring and summer of 1938.[51] Given the refusal of Britain and France to join the Soviet Union in specific negotiations on the maintenance of Czechoslovakian security, the centre of interest lay in the question of whether France and the Soviet Union would fulfil their commitments to render military assistance to Czechoslovakia in the event of a German seizure of the Sudetenland. Throughout this period successive senior Soviet spokesmen, including Kalinin, Litvinov and Troyanovsky, the Soviet Ambassador to the United States, reaffirmed the determination of the Soviet Union to assist Czechoslovakia in the event of war.[52] It was emphasised, however, that Soviet assistance by the terms of the existing treaties was conditional on France also providing direct assistance. From the outset, therefore, the key to the situation lay in the attitude adopted by the French government. Whilst the emphasis placed upon a prior French commitment to assist in the defence of Czechoslovakia placed a question mark against the role that the Soviet Union would play in the event of German aggression it has been subsequently claimed that, confidentially, the Czechoslovak government was repeatedly assured that the Red Army and the Red Airforce would respond immediately if the Czechoslovaks elected to resist a German invasion. It has been suggested that Marshal Kulik, head of the Soviet military delegation that visited Czechoslovakia in March 1938, assured his Czech counterpart, General Krejci, that the Red Army would assist in the defence of the Czechoslovakian state.[53] In addition, the leader of the Czechoslovakian Communist Party, Gottwald, later claimed that he passed a personal message from Stalin to the Czechoslovakian Premier, Beneš, declaring that:

> the Soviet Union was prepared to render military assistance to Czechoslovakia even if France refused to do so which was a condition of Soviet aid, and even if Poland of the Beck Government or Rumania of the boyars refused to allow Soviet troops to pass through. Naturally, stressed Stalin, the Soviet Union could render assistance to Czechoslovakia on the sole condition that Czechoslovakia would defend herself and request Soviet aid.[54]

While the above pledges of aid to the Czechoslovaks are difficult to substantiate, it is undeniable that throughout the crisis Litvinov continued to emphasise that the Soviet Union would fulfil its treaty commitments to Czechoslovakia.[55] At the height of the crisis, on 21 September, the Commissar for Foreign Affairs reaffirmed his country's dedication to the cause of collective security:

> We intend to fulfil our obligations under the pact and, together with France, to afford assistance to Czechoslovakia by the ways open to us. Our War Department is ready immediately to participate in a conference with representatives of the French and Czechoslovak War Department in order to discuss the measures appropriate to the moment. Independently of this we should consider it desirable that the question be raised at the League of Nations, if only as yet under Article 11, with the object first, of mobilising public opinion and, secondly, of ascertaining the position of certain other States, whose passive aid might be extremely valuable. It was necessary, however, to exhaust all means of averting an armed conflict, and we considered one such method to be an immediate consultation between the Great Powers of Europe and other interested States, in order if possible to decide on the terms of a collective *démarche*.[56]

This statement was followed two days later by a warning to the Polish government that, in the event of a Polish attempt to occupy Czechoslovakian territory, the Soviet Union would feel compelled to denounce the Soviet–Polish pact of non-aggression.[57] In addition, pledges of military assistance were repeated confidentially to France and Czechoslovakia. On 25 September, the Commissar for Defence informed the French government that the Red Army had moved 30 infantry divisions to its western borders and the Red Airforce had concentrated 246 bombers and 302 fighter aircraft in the Kiev and Byelorussian districts for despatch to Czechoslovakia.[58] In response to the problem of gaining transit for the Red Army through either Rumania or Poland both Litvinov and Potemkin, Vice-Commissar for Foreign Affairs, informed the French *chargé d'affaires* in Moscow that they believed this could be engineered through the offices of the League of Nations if Czechoslovakia was to invoke the Covenant of the League in its defence.[59] Further reassurance was given to the Czechoslovakian government on 20 September 1938, when, in response to a question by Beneš, the Soviet Ambassador in Prague, Alexandrovsky, was authorised by Litvinov to give the following reply:

> 1. To Beneš' question, whether or not the USSR (in accord with the treaty) will give immediate and effective assistance to Czechoslovakia if France also remains true to Czechoslovakia and gives her assistance, you may give, on behalf of the Soviet Government, an affirmative reply.
> 2. You may also give an affirmative reply to Beneš' other question on whether or not the USSR will help Czechoslovakia, as a member of the League of Nations on the basis of clauses 16 and 17 if, in the event of attack by Germany, Beneš requests the League Council to invoke these clauses.[60]

Given these statements it might well be seen as surprising that Beneš capitulated to the terms devised at the Munich meeting which involved the loss of 20 per cent of Czechoslovakian territory and 25 per cent of its population.[61] In addition, any suggestion of direct or indirect resistance to the German demands through either the use of the well-equipped Czechoslovakian army or recourse to the League of Nations appeared to have been discounted. It seemed that not only were the Soviet guarantees to Czechoslovakia brushed aside but, as the events at Munich indicated, Britain and France strove throughout the crisis to exclude the Soviet Union from all deliberations on the Czechoslovakian question. In attempting to defend this stance it was argued that there was a strong case for the reunification of the Sudetenland with Germany given the size of the German speaking population in the region.[62] This argument was repeatedly expounded in elements of the British press. On 22 March 1938, *The Times* first challenged the suggestion that German claims should be arbitrarily denied:

> If we were to involve ourselves in war to preserve Czech sovereignty over these Germans without firstly clearly ascertaining their wishes, we might well be fighting against the principle of self determination.[63]

At the height of the crisis, on 7 September 1938, *The Times* once again questioned the logic behind the retention in Czechoslovakia of the 'fringe of alien populations who are contiguous to the nation to which they are united by race'.[64] The conviction that, in principle, Hitler had a strong case for the unification of the Sudetenland with the German Reich was not confined solely to the British press. As early as November 1937, Chamberlain had informed the French Premier, Chautemps, and his Foreign Secretary, Delbos, that Britain would not fight to defend Czechoslovakian domination of the Sudetenland and that steps must be taken to increase the autonomy of the Sudeten Germans.[65]

Given that there were serious doubts as to the wisdom of denying Germany the Sudetenland the dilemma confronting the British and French governments in the summer of 1938 was further deepened by a stream of military assessments that adopted a largely pessimistic view of the preparedness of their armed forces for a European war. On 14 September the British Chiefs of Staff reported:

> no pressure Great Britain and France can bring to bear either by sea, land or in the air, could prevent Germany from over-running Bohemia and from inflicting a decisive defeat on Czechoslovakia. The restoration of Czechoslovakia could only be achieved by the defeat of Germany, and as the outcome of prolonged struggle which from the outset must assume the character of an unlimited war.[66]

This report was followed, on 22 September, by a Note from General Ismay, Secretary to the Committee of Imperial Defence, stating that: 'from the military point of view it would be better to fight her [Germany] in say 6-12 months time than to accept the present challenge'.[67] General Ismay's conclusions were undoubtedly influenced by the belief that few nations would join Britain and France in military measures to deny Germany the Sudetenland. In particular, Ismay was aware that South Africa and Canada had joined the United States of America in urging Britain and France to seek a peaceful solution of the problem.[68]

Military action against Germany, however, hinged initially upon collaboration between France and the Soviet Union. Despite repeated assurances that the Red Army was prepared to act alongside the French to uphold their joint treaty commitments to defend Czechoslovakia, the French government candidly expressed to its British counterpart its scepticism as to the Red Army's ability to fulfil this pledge.[69] On 15 March 1938, the Committee of National Defence noted the absence of military contingency planning behind the façade of the Franco–Soviet and Czechoslovak–Soviet treaties of mutual assistance and expressed grave reservations as to the ability of the Red Army to render effective aid to Czechoslovakia.[70] As a result of this report, in April 1938 the French informed the British that they had little faith in the military capability of the Red Army. This assessment was corroborated by a stream of French military intelligence reports compiled during the summer.[71] The situation was further compounded by the reluctance of either Poland or Rumania to grant transit facilities for the Red Army to cross their territory *en route* to Czechoslovakia.[72] It was evident that the east European nations had no intention of allowing the Red Army onto their soil.[73] Fear of Soviet motives was almost certainly an influential factor in Czech considerations. Dr Hubert Ripka later claimed:

> To ask help from Soviet Russia alone would have been dangerous from internal Czechoslovak reasons also, for although all our political parties were united in favour of seeking help from France and Russia combined, the parties of the Right would certainly have protested against accepting help from Russia alone.[74]

A report from the Soviet Ambassador to Prague, Alexandrovsky, certainly suggested that Beneš was reluctant to call upon military assistance from the Soviet Union:

> I have no doubt that this dry pedant and shrewd diplomat from start to finish has hoped to achieve the maximum possible for Czechoslovakia through British and French support and only regards Soviet assistance, from the point of view of the Czechoslovak bourgeoisie, as an extremely suicidal means of defending Czechoslovakia from Hitler's attacks.[75]

It would appear, therefore, that there was little enthusiasm in Paris, London or Prague for a confrontation with Germany over the Sudetenland issue, and even less confidence in the ability — and, indeed, in the desirability — of the Red Army playing a prominent role in a European war. The decision to identify Czechoslovakia as primarily a European affair and effectively to exclude the Soviet

Union from deliberations on European matters had been taken by Chamberlain in November 1937.[76] On 20 March 1938, he outlined his reasons for seeking to avoid a major clash over the future of Czechoslovakia:

> with Franco winning in Spain by the aid of German guns and Italian planes, with a French Government in which one cannot have the slighest confidence and which I suspect to be in closish touch with our Opposition, with Russia stealthily and cunningly pulling all the strings behind the scenes to get us involved in war with Germany (our Secret Service doesn't spend all its time looking out of the window) and finally with a Germany flushed with triumph and all too conscious of her power, the prospect looked black indeed.
>
> You have only to look at the map to see that nothing that France or we could do could possibly save Czechoslovakia from being over-run by the Germans, if they wanted to do it.
>
> . . . she [Czechoslovakia] would simply be a pretext for going to war with Germany.
>
> I have therefore abandoned any idea of giving guarantees to Czechoslovakia, or the French in connection with her obligations to that country.[77]

Behind this statement lay the logic of Munich. For Chamberlain and Daladier the Czechoslovak crisis was primarily a European affair and, therefore, the primary concern of Britain, France, Germany and Italy. The decision to ostracise the Soviet Union was based initially on a general suspicion of Soviet and communist ambitions in Eastern and Central Europe. This concern was subsequently reinforced by the hostility evinced by the East European powers to any suggestion of their being manoeuvred into a relationship with the Soviet Union that would facilitate the establishment of a Soviet military or political presence in Eastern Europe. It appeared, therefore, that there were grounds to suspect that the embrace of fascist Germany was more attractive to the smaller nations than the possibility of absorption into the communist sphere of influence. In this light it was not altogether surprising that Britain and France were reluctant to accede to Soviet demands that pressure be imposed on Poland and Rumania to grant transit facilities to the Red Army.[78]

Behind this general suspicion of the Soviet Union lay Chamberlain's conviction that the central problem in the stabilisation of European security was the attainment of an agreement on armament levels and collective security with Germany.[79] In this sense, as the Czechoslovakian crisis developed in the summer of 1938, Chamberlain was prepared to agree to the transfer of the Sudetenland to the German

Reich if the settlement incorporated the basis for a wider understanding between Britain, France and Germany.[80] In this context the return of the German-speaking districts to the German Reich was seen by the British government as both a reasonable settlement of a dispute in which they had little desire to be embroiled, and a promising departure point for a broad agreement with Germany.[81] The significance attached by Chamberlain to the settlement was indicated by his determination to conduct the negotiations with Hitler in person which led to a series of meetings at Berchtesgaden, Godesberg and Munich in September 1938. The Munich agreement was, therefore, seen as a major success for the Prime Minister in that it settled the Sudeten question without recourse to war and established the basis for an international security settlement with Germany. The German Ambassador in London had little doubt that the general settlement was of primary importance to the British government:

> [HMG] were secretly glad that as a result of the Munich Conference, Czechoslovakia was no longer the bone of contention. They regarded the protocol signed by the Fuhrer and Chamberlain in Munich as a new basis and guideline for developing Anglo–German relations as 'peace in our time'. Their belief in the possibility of settling differences and easing the tension was based on this.[82]

In this context Chamberlain attempted to play down the sacrifices imposed upon the Czechoslovakians and pointed to the contribution that the Munich agreement had made to world peace. On 2 October 1938, the Prime Minister wrote to the Archbishop of Canterbury:

> I am sure that some day the Czechs will see that what we did was to save them for a happier future. And I sincerely believe that we have at last opened the way to that general appeasement which alone can save the world from chaos.[83]

Chamberlain was subsequently to claim that the speed of events in September 1938 precluded full discussion of the Czechoslovakian situation with the Soviet Union and, indeed, made it impossible for the Soviet Union to be invited to attend the Munich conference despite its treaty commitments to Czechoslovakia.[84] It would appear that Litvinov's brief discussion with Earl de la Warr, the Lord Privy Seal, on 23 September 1938, at Geneva, was the sole instance of direct Anglo–Soviet negotiation on the Czechoslovak situation throughout the crisis.[85] In reality, however, Chamberlain made a positive decision to exclude the Soviet Union from all negotiations. Not only did the Prime Minister hold reservations as to the desirability of involving the Soviet Union in Eastern European affairs but he was also convinced that the Czechoslovakian matter was one that could be settled quite satisfactorily between Britain, France, Germany and Italy. In essence, Chamberlain saw the involvement of the Soviet Union, at its best, as largely irrelevant and, at its worst, as counter-productive given Hitler's hostility to communism and the Soviet Union.[86] Indeed, as part of the Munich settlement, steps were taken to cut the links between Czechoslovakia and the Soviet Union with the proposal that Czechoslovakia's existing security agreements be superseded by a broad international guarantee of its future status.[87] If further evidence was necessary the Munich agreement emphasised that Britain and France had no intention of allowing the Soviet Union to participate in European affairs and clearly saw the basis of collective security as revolving around an understanding between Paris, London and Berlin.

As might have been anticipated the reaction of the Soviet press to the Munich agreement was prompt and highly critical. On 4 October 1938, *Izvestia* declared:

> the so-called democratic countries' capitulation to the aggressor, seeming to reduce the possibility of war, in fact makes it more likely and besides immeasurably worsens the situation for Britain and France.[88]

Pravda argued that the agreement represented a betrayal by Britain and France of both Czechoslovakia and the cause of collective security:

> All the peoples of the world can clearly see that behind the smokescreen of fine phrases about Chamberlain having saved the world peace at Munich, an act has been committed which by its shamelessness has surpassed all that has taken place since the first imperialist war.[89]

In effect, the Soviet Union wiped its hands of the Czechoslovakian question and vigorously denied that it had played any part in the formulation of the Munich agreement. In response to a press report that the Soviet Union had been consulted prior to the Munich conference and had agreed that its interests be represented by the French Premier, Daladier, *Tass* replied on 4 October:

> No conversations were held, still less any agreements made, between the Soviet, French and English Governments on the fate of the Czechoslovak Republic and concessions to the aggressor. Neither France nor England consulted the USSR, but only informed the Soviet Government of *faits accomplis*. As already made clear in the Tass statement of 2 October, the Soviet Government had and has nothing whatever to do with the Munich conference and its decisions.[90]

It would appear reasonable to assume that the Munich conference signalled the final collapse of the Soviet Union's attempts to forge a relationship with Britain and France to uphold the status quo in Europe.[91] Max Beloff has argued that Munich was, therefore, a major turning-point in the course of interwar Soviet foreign policy in that it

> was sufficient to dispel most of the remaining hold which the 'collective security' idea may have had in Soviet circles, and it is obvious that the retreat into isolation now gathered further momentum.[92]

In support of this argument Beloff quoted James Brynes, the United States Secretary of State, who recorded, of a conversation with Stalin in 1945, that the Soviet leader admitted that it was the failure to consult the Soviet Union over the Czechoslovakian issue that forced the Soviet leadership to reassess relations with Britain and France and to move away from the principle of collective security to a position of neutrality.[93] Undeniably, following the Munich agreement, a new tone was discernible in official Soviet policy statements. Molotov, in a survey of the international situation delivered on 6 November 1938, made a sweeping assault on the policies of Britain and France:

> The French and English Governments sacrificed not only Czechoslovakia but their own interests as well, for the sake of an agreement with the aggressors.
>
> The bargain between the fascist governments and the governments of the so-called democratic countries, far from lessening the danger of the outbreak of the second imperialist war, has on the contrary added fuel to the flames.[94]

Molotov emphasised that the Soviet Union had taken no part in the betrayal of Czechoslovakia:

> The Soviet Union did not and could not take part in the bargaining of the imperialists, of the fascists and so-called democratic governments at the expense of Czechoslovakia. The Soviet Union did not and could not take part in the dismemberment of Czechoslovakia to satisfy the appetites of German fascism and its allies. No doubt can remain about Soviet policy on this question.[95]

In pointing to the threat that still existed to 'certain other European countries', Molotov no longer called upon the League of Nations to champion the cause of collective security but fell back upon the argument that the Soviet Union did not need allies in order to repulse any military challenge that might be made to its future territorial integrity.[96] Molotov's words implied that the Soviet Union had rejected the policy of collaboration with Britain and France in favour of a return to a position of self-sufficiency. In resurrecting the image of the Soviet Union as a socialist island in a hostile international environment Molotov appeared to be turning the clock back a decade. Yet he was not alone in assuming this stance, for in this period the Comintern once again began to refer to a capitalist conspiracy to overthrow the Soviet Union. In its assessment of the Munich agreement the Comintern argued that the settlement was indicative of an Anglo–French design to use Germany as a tool to crush communism: 'The British and French reactionaries need fascist dictators as bloody gendarmes for the battle against the international working class and the world democratic movement.'[97]

Certainly, this fear was not completely unfounded for in the months following the Munich settlement Britain and France appeared content to consolidate their position in Western Europe at the expense of East European economic and political independence. On 15 November the British Foreign Secretary, Lord Halifax, informed the Rumanian Foreign Minister that it was no part of British policy to obstruct German economic expansion in Eastern Europe.[98] In the same month the French government was told that Britain had no intention of providing an unconditional guarantee of future Czechoslovakian territorial integrity. This statement effectively destroyed any hope that might have existed of the guarantees incorporated within the Munich agreement being fulfilled.[99] Anglo–French ambitions appeared to be firmly set on a settlement of outstanding differences with Germany and progress seemed to have been made with the Franco–German Declaration of 6 December 1938,[100] which paralleled the terms of the Anglo–German Declaration of 30 September 1938. A further source of irritation was resolved on 27 February 1939 when Britain and France formally recognised Franco's regime as the legitimate government of Spain.[101]

In such a climate Hitler needed little encouragement to seek further expansion of the German sphere of influence in Eastern Europe. The destabilisation of the Czechoslovakian state was continued with the promotion of separatist movements in Ruthenia and Slovakia.[102] In addition, the German Foreign Minister, Joachim von Ribbentrop, held a series of meetings with the Polish Foreign Minister, Beck, and the Polish Ambassador to Berlin, Lipski, at which demands for the cession to Germany of the port of Danzig and a rail- and road-link through Polish territory were expounded.[103] Alongside this campaign Hitler continued to stress his commitment to the containment of communism. In October 1938, as a result of German pressure, the Communist Party was banned in Moravia and Bohemia, and on 24 February 1939, Hungary joined the Anti-Comintern pact.[104] Of even more concern to the Soviet Union, however, was the establishment in October 1938 of an autonomous Ruthenian state within Czechoslovakia. It was evident that Hitler saw Ruthenia — or Carpatho–Ukraine as it was renamed in January 1939 — as the focus of a campaign to ignite the forces of Ukrainian nationalism. It was evident that such a movement would seek ultimately to detach the prosperous Ukrainian provinces incorporated within Poland and the Soviet Union.[105]

The challenge presented by a German-sponsored Ukrainian separatist movement was one that the Soviet Union could not ignore. It was significant that Stalin, in his report to the Eighteenth Congress of the CPSU, went to great lengths to dismiss the possibility of the Soviet Ukraine being detached from the Soviet Union:

> It is quite possible, of course, that there are madmen in Germany who dream of annexing the elephant, that is, the Soviet Ukraine, to the gnat, namely, the so-called Carpathian Ukraine. If there really are such lunatics in Germany, rest assured that we shall find enough straitjackets for them in our country.[106]

While clearly identifying Germany, Japan and Italy as the aggressor states within the international system, Stalin was equally scathing in his references to Britain and France which he claimed had: 'rejected the policy of collective security, the policy of collective resistance to aggressors, and have taken up the position of non-intervention, a position of "neutrality".'[107] This stance, he argued, was based upon the assumption that Anglo–French interests could be protected by encouraging Germany and Japan to satisfy their appetites at the expense of the Soviet Union and China.[108] With this denunciation of Anglo–French policy, Stalin indicated that he saw military strength rather than international collaboration as the cornerstone of Soviet foreign policy:[109] 'We are not afraid of the threats of aggressors, and are ready to deal two blows for every blow delivered by instigators of war who attempt to violate the Soviet borders.'[110] Furthermore, he served notice that Britain and France could no longer expect automatic support for their attempts to counter German ambitions. The Soviet leader declared that, in the future, Soviet foreign policy would be 'cautious and not allow our country to be drawn into conflicts by warmongers who are accustomed to have others pull the chestnuts out of the fire for them.'[111]

With this speech Stalin appeared finally to have turned his back on the League of Nations in favour of bolstering Soviet military strength as a deterrent to aggression. In addition, in the following months, the Soviet Union sought to improve links with its East European neighbours.[112] With the loss of Czechoslovakia's key western fortification system to Germany the maintenance of Polish independence assumed a central position in Soviet strategy.[113] The Czechoslovakian crisis had produced a dramatic deterioration in Soviet–Polish relations as a result of a Soviet threat to abrogate the Soviet–Polish non-aggression treaty if the Poles occupied the Czechoslovakian district of Teschen.[114] Although the Soviet Union and Poland stood on the brink of war in September 1938, in the months following the Munich settlement it was evident that, with German sponsorship of the Ukrainian nationalist movement and the growing demand for the surrender of Danzig, both states shared a common interest in resisting any further German encroachments in Eastern Europe.[115] On this basis a tacit Soviet–Polish understanding was established, and the relationship was cemented by the signing on 26 November 1938 of a protocol extending the pact of non-aggression for a further seven years, followed by the conclusion of a commercial agreement on 17 February 1939.[116]

While attempting to bolster his western frontiers, Stalin also sought once again to utilise the remaining economic and commercial ties with Germany as a vehicle for a regeneration of relations with Hitler.[117] Yet despite the conclusion of a trade and payments agreement in December 1938, and the promise of further trade discussions in Moscow in the spring of 1939,[118] the sudden cancellation of the negotiations indicated that Hitler saw little immediate advantage in improving relations.[119]

The attempt to resuscitate Soviet–German links can perhaps be seen as a product of the Munich agreement and the failure of collective security.[120] Yet it is difficult to see Munich as a major turning-point in Soviet foreign policy, for it would seem more realistic to admit that the Soviet commitment to Geneva was conditioned by Stalin's determination to defuse the threat posed to Soviet territorial integrity by the demands emanating from Berlin and Tokyo. It was both logical and consistent with previous policy to seek an understanding with Japan and Germany which might deflect their ambitions away from the borders of the Soviet Union. In this context it is possible to contend that attempts to seek a political alignment with Germany in the months following the Munich agreement did not represent a readjustment of the Soviet stance but merely a continuation of a policy that had been an important strand of Soviet strategy for over a decade.[121]

Undoubtedly, however, the Austrian and Czechoslovakian crises had led the Soviet Union to review the nature of its relationship with Britain and France. The downgrading of the significance of links with London and Paris was suggested by the Soviet response to the Munich agreement which accused the western powers of surrendering to German demands and seeking to safeguard their interests by tacitly giving Germany a free hand in Eastern Europe. Furthermore, repeated Soviet allusions to the development of its military strength to a level at which its defensive capability outstripped that of any potential aggressor seemed indicative of a general indifference to future links with the western powers.[122] In November 1936 Litvinov had declared that Soviet policy was not dependent on alliances or links with any of the major powers:

> The Soviet Union, however, does not beg to be invited to any unions, any blocs, any combinations. She will calmly let other States weigh and evaluate the advantages which can be derived for peace from close co-operation with the Soviet Union and understand that the Soviet Union can give more than receive.[123]

On 16 October 1938, Litvinov reaffirmed this stance:

> Henceforth the USSR has only to watch from the shelters of its frontiers, the establishment of German hegemony over the centre and south-east of Europe. And if by chance the Western Powers finally decided to wish to stop it, they must address themselves to us, for . . . we shall have our word to say.[124]

Yet it would be dangerous to exaggerate the extent of the disaffection generated by the Munich agreement. Certainly there was no suggestion of a Soviet determination to quit the League. At the height of the Czechoslovakian crisis Litvinov had emphasised the Soviet Union's dedication to the cause of collective security:

> The Soviet Union takes pride in the fact that it has no part in such a policy, and has invariably pursued the principle of the two pacts I have mentioned which were approved by nearly every nation in the world. Nor has it any intention of abandoning them for the future, being convinced that in present conditions it is impossible otherwise to safeguard a genuine peace and genuine international justice. It calls upon other Governments likewise to return to this path.[125]

Furthermore, in March 1939 Stalin indicated that Soviet policy still saw a positive role for the League of Nations in preserving peace: 'The Soviet Union considers that in alarming times like these even so weak an international organisation as the League of Nations should not be ignored.'[126] It appeared, therefore, that while the Soviet Union remained outwardly indifferent to the value of reasserting relations with Britain and France, the possibility of such a course of action was not entirely discounted. In an attempt to underline their common interest in restraining German ambitions, Litvinov continued to warn the French government that Hitler sought to dominate both Western and Eastern Europe.[127] In March 1939 the Soviet Commissar underlined his concern in conversation with a representative of the British Embassy. The official later recorded that Litvinov

> foresaw in the not far distant future a Europe entirely German from the Bay of Biscay to the Soviet frontier and bounded, as it were, simply by Great Britain and the Soviet Union. Even that would not satisfy German ambition, but the attack, he said, smiling happily, would not be directed to the east.[128]

In addition there is little doubt that observers at the German Embassy in Moscow suspected that Litvinov was anxious to rebuild links with Paris and London in an attempt to encircle Germany. In October 1938 von Tippelskirch reported to the German Foreign Ministry:

> Litvinov will certainly try to convince the Soviet Government that the policy hitherto pursued by him was the only right one and that it must be continued in the future as well. . . . If I judge Litvinov correctly, he will continue to defend his policy of collective action in the conviction that Germany's growth of power . . . will lead to a change in the European balance of power in which sooner or later a definite role must quite automatically fall to the Soviet Union.
>
> In other words he will continue to recommend measures against the aggressors in the hope of having more success next time.[129]

It would seem, therefore, that although the post-Munich period witnessed a noticeable cooling in relations with the western powers, there was no suggestion of any desire to break the links established with Paris, London or Geneva. The fact that the Soviet Union chose to remain within the League of Nations, despite its abject failure to counter numerous flagrant breaches of international law, was indicative of the belief that membership of the League was still of value to the Soviet state. Not only was the League seen as a deterrent to the expansionist ambitions of Japan and Germany but, in addition, it solidified the division of the capitalist powers into two competing factions and therefore diminished the possibility of a concerted effort by the western powers to destroy the heart of the communist revolution.

In this sense the limited goals assigned to relations with Britain and France within the framework of collective security were still valid in the months following the Munich settlement. Indeed the effective nullification of Czechoslovakian military potential had increased the immediate threat to the continued independence of the Eastern European nations separating the Soviet Union and Germany. Given the evidence of a German determination to draw Poland and Rumania into the Nazi sphere of influence the threat to Soviet territorial integrity was implicit. While Hitler remained unresponsive to Soviet overtures, Stalin had no option but to continue his search for an agreement or understanding with those nations with a common interest in restraining German ambitions. In this context behind the declarations of military strength, Stalin appreciated that the tide in Eastern Europe was running against the Soviet Union. Despite his contempt for the western powers and his suspicion of their motives, Stalin realised that the Munich agreement had actually increased his need to pursue an alliance with Britain and France.[130]

Notes

1. Jane Degras (ed.), *Soviet Documents on Foreign Policy*. Vol. 3: *1933–1941* (New York, 1978), Election speech by Litvinov on the international situation, Leningrad, 27 November 1937, pp. 266-8.
2. Ibid., p. 267.
3. Ibid., p. 266.
4. Ibid., p. 267.
5. Ibid.
6. Ibid., p. 268.
7. Degras, Extracts from a speech by the Soviet Ambassador in London on the war danger, London, 9 March 1936, pp. 178-82.
8. Ibid., Speech by Litvinov on the report of the League of Nations to the Eighteenth Assembly, Geneva, 21 September 1937, p. 262.
9. Ibid., pp. 260-1.
10. Ibid., p. 257.
11. Joseph E. Davies, *Mission to Moscow* (London, 1944), p. 49.
12. See ibid., pp. 61, 80, 92.
13. Ibid., p. 165.
14. Degras, Speech by the Soviet Ambassador in London on the war danger, London, 13 March 1937, pp. 236-8.
15. Ibid., Open letter by Stalin on the position of the Soviet state in a capitalist encirclement, 12 February 1938, pp. 273-5.
16. Compare Stalin's analysis of 12 February 1938, with Litvinov's of 29 December 1933, in ibid., pp. 48-61.
17. Ibid., pp. 130-2.
18. Arnold Wolfers, *Britain and France Between Two Wars* (New York, 1966), pp. 136-41. See also J. Nere, *The Foreign Policy of France from 1914 to 1945* (London, 1975); and Arthur H. Furnia, *The Diplomacy of Appeasement. Anglo–French Relations and the Prelude to World War II, 1931–1938* (Washington, D.C., 1960).
19. Anthony Eden, *The Eden Memoirs*. Vol. 1: *Facing the Dictators* (London, 1962), pp. 144-63.

20. Ibid., p. 162.
21. For examples see Nere, p. 164; and Sir John Simon, *Retrospect* (London, 1952), p. 203.
22. Monica Curtis (ed.), *Documents on International Affairs*. Vol. I: *1938* (London, 1942), Speech by Rt Hon. Neville Chamberlain in the House of Commons, 21 February 1938, pp. 16-24.
23. K. Feiling, *The Life of Neville Chamberlain* (London, 1946), pp. 333-4. See also John E. Dreifort, *Yvon Delbos at the Quai d'Orsay* (University of Kansas Press, 1973), pp. 105-24.
24. Albert Seaton, *Stalin and the Red Army General Staff in the Thirties,* in Adrian Preston, *General Staffs and Diplomacy before the Second World War* (London, 1978), pp. 65-76.
25. Davies, p. 116.
26. D. C. Watt, 'Soviet Military Aid to the Spanish Revolution in the Spanish Civil War, 1936–1938', *Slovanic and East European Review,* June 1960.
27. For example, see Hitler's conversation with the British Ambassador to Berlin, Henderson, of 3 March 1938, contained in *Documents and Materials Relating to the Eve of the Second World War.* Vol. I (Moscow, 1948), pp. 50-67.
28. See Gerhard L. Weinberg, *The Foreign Policy of Hitler's Germany.* Vol. I: *Diplomatic Revolution in Europe, 1933–1936* (University of Chicago Press, 1970), pp. 12-13, 75-6.
29. Max Beloff, *The Foreign Policy of Soviet Russia.* Vol. II: *1936–1941* (London, 1949), pp. 72-83.
30. Quoted in Feiling, pp. 322-4.
31. *Documents and Materials,* Conversation between Hitler and Halifax, 19 November 1937, pp. 13-45.
32. Ibid.
33. Feiling, pp. 332-3.
34. *Documents and Materials,* Conversation between Hitler and Henderson, 3 March 1938, pp. 50-67.
35. Ibid., p. 63.
36. Curtis, pp. 137-55. Also Jill Edwards, *The British Government and the Spanish Civil War* (London, 1979), pp. 132-80.
37. See Eden, pp. 586-606; Feiling, pp. 329-42.
38. Quoted in Feiling, p. 337.
39. Gerhard L. Weinberg, *The Foreign Policy of Hitler's Germany.* Vol. 2: *Starting World War II 1937–1939* (University of Chicago Press, 1980), pp. 264-312.
40. Quoted in Beloff, p. 121.
41. *Documents and Materials,* Conversation between Hitler and Henderson, 3 March 1938, pp. 50-67.
42. Davies, p. 165.
43. *Pravda,* 28 September 1937, quoted in I. K. Koblyakov, *USSR: For Peace Against Aggression, 1933–1941* (Moscow, 1976), p. 85.
44. Koblyakov, pp. 85-6.

45. Degras, Press statement by Litvinov on the International situation after the incorporation of Austria in Germany, 17 March 1938, pp. 276-7.
46. Ibid.
47. Beloff, p. 123.
48. *Documents and Materials,* Note from British Foreign Office to the Soviet Embassy in London, 24 March 1938, pp. 89-92.
49. Davies, p. 194.
50. Ibid., pp. 189-90.
51. *Documents and Materials,* Minutes of a conference on the Sudetenland presided over by Ribbentrop, 29 March 1938, pp. 93-9. See also Beloff, pp. 125-6.
52. See Degras, pp. 279, 282-94; and Curtis, p. 315.
53. Koblyakov, pp. 89-91.
54. K. Gottwald, *For a Lasting Peace, for a People's Democracy* (21 December 1949), quoted in Koblyakov, p. 90.
55. Degras, pp. 282-94, 299-304.
56. Ibid., Speech by Litvinov at the League of Nations Assembly, Geneva, 21 September 1938, pp. 299-304.
57. Ibid., Statement by Vice-Commissar Potemkin to the Polish chargé d'affaires in Moscow, 23 September 1938, p. 305.
58. Koblyakov, pp. 106-97.
59. Ibid., p. 104; see also Beloff, p. 143; and Degras, pp. 299-304.
60. Quoted in Koblyakov, p. 108.
61. *Documents and Materials,* Test of the Munich Agreement, 29 September 1938, pp. 244-55.
62. See Feiling, pp. 333-4, 363-4.
63. *The Times,* 22 March 1938.
64. Ibid., 7 September 1938.
65. Feiling, pp. 333-4.
66. Quoted in Stephen Roskill, *Hankey, Man of Secrets.* Vol. III: *1931–1963* (London, 1974), p. 379.
67. Quoted in Roskill, p. 380.
68. Ibid., pp. 382-8.
69. Dreifort, pp. 116-23.
70. Beloff, pp. 126-7.
71. Ibid., pp. 127-8.
72. Adam B. Ulam, *Expansion and Coexistence. The History of Soviet Foreign Policy, 1917–1967* (London, 1968), pp. 254-5.
73. Ibid., p. 255.
74. H. Ripka, *Munich: Before and After* (London, 1939), pp. 85-7.
75. Quoted in Koblyakov, p. 90.
76. Feiling, pp. 333-4.
77. Quoted in Feiling, pp. 347-8.
78. Koblyakov, pp. 110-16.
79. Feiling, pp. 347-8.
80. See Koblyakov, pp. 97-8.
81. Weinberg, Vol. II, pp. 392-3.

82. Quoted in Koblyakov, p. 111.
83. Quoted in Feiling, p. 375.
84. Ibid., pp. 375-6.
85. Beloff, p. 157.
86. Feiling, pp. 347-8.
87. *Documents and Materials,* Text of the Munich Agreement, 29 September 1938, pp. 244-55.
88. Quoted in Koblyakov, p. 112.
89. Ibid., p. 111.
90. Degras, p. 307. *Tass* statement, 4 October 1938.
91. See F. L. Schuman, *Europe on the Eve* (London, 1942), pp. 442-56; and Wolfers, pp. 304-10.
92. Beloff, p. 166.
93. J. F. Brynes, *Speaking Frankly* (London, 1947), p. 283. Quoted in Beloff, p. 165.
94. Degras, Speech by Molotov on the international situation, 6 November 1938, pp. 308-11.
95. Ibid., p. 310.
96. Ibid., p. 311.
97. Georgi Dimitrov, *The Earnest of Victory* (Moscow, 1938), p. 6.
98. Koblyakov, p. 117.
99. See Feiling, pp. 333-4; and Gerhard L. Weinberg, *Germany and the Soviet Union, 1939–1941* (Leiden, 1954), p. 4.
100. *Documents and Materials,* Franco–German Declaration, 6 December 1938, pp. 284-5.
101. Beloff, p. 219.
102. Ibid., pp. 213-17.
103. Louis Fischer, *Russia's Road from Peace to War* (New York, 1969), p. 323.
104. Beloff, pp. 213-17.
105. Ibid., pp. 213-18.
106. Degras, Stalin's report to the Eighteenth Congress of the CPSU, 10 March 1939, pp. 315-22.
107. Ibid., p. 318.
108. Ibid., p. 319.
109. Ibid., Speech by Molotov on the international situation, 6 November 1938, pp. 308-11.
110. Ibid., p. 321.
111. Ibid., p. 322.
112. Ibid., p. 321.
113. See S. H. Haigh, D. S. Morris and A. R. Peters, 'European Rearmament Policies and their Effect on the Balance of Military Power from Munich 1938 to the Outbreak of War 1939', Sheffield City Polytechnic, Department of Political Studies Occasional Paper, Molotov–Ribbentrop Pact No. 10.
114. Degras, Statement by Vice-Commissar Potemkin to the Polish chargé d'affaires in Moscow, September 1938, p. 305.
115. Fischer, pp. 322-3.

116. Ibid. See also Degras, *Tass* communiqué conversations between the Foreign Commissar and Polish Ambassador in Moscow, 27 November 1938, p. 312.
117. For an outline of German–Soviet economic relations, see Gustav Hilger and Alfred G. Meyer, *The Incompatible Allies* (New York, 1971), pp. 165-86, 288-340.
118. Weinberg, *Germany and the Soviet Union,* p. 11.
119. Ibid., pp. 10-13.
120. Ibid., p. 7. See also R. H. Haigh, D. S. Morris and A. R. Peters, 'The Unconsidered Ally: Britain, the USSR and Appeasement', Sheffield City Polytechnic, Department of Political Studies Occasional Paper, Molotov–Ribbentrop Pact No. 3.
121. See A. R. Peters, R. H. Haigh and D. S. Morris, 'In Search of Peace: The Soviet Union and the League of Nations 1919–1934', Sheffield City Polytechnic, Department of Political Studies Occasional Paper, Molotov–Ribbentrop Pact No. 8.
122. See Degras, Speech by Molotov, 6 November 1938, pp. 308-11; Stalin's Report to the Eighteenth Congress of the CPSU, 10 March 1939, pp. 315-22.
123. Ibid., Litvinov's speech at the Eighth (Extraordinary) Soviet Congress, 28 November 1936, pp. 220-6.
124. *Soviet Peace Efforts on the Eve of World War Two. Documents and Records.* Vol. I (Moscow, 1973), Memorandum of conversation between Litvinov and the French Ambassador in USSR, 16 October 1938, pp. 63-5.
125. Degras, Speech by Litvinov at the League of Nations Assembly, 21 September 1938, pp. 299-304.
126. Ibid., Stalin's report to the Eighteenth Congress of the CPSU, 10 March 1939, pp. 315-22.
127. *Soviet Peace Efforts,* 16 October 1938, pp. 63-5; 20 November 1938, pp. 103-4.
128. Ibid., Statement by Litvinov to British Parliamentary Secretary of the Department of Overseas Trade, 23 March 1939, pp. 280-2.
129. *Documents on German Foreign Policy, 1918–1945,* Series D, Vol. IV, pp. 602-5.
130. For a broad discussion of this argument, see Adam B. Ulam, *Expansion and Coexistence* (London, 1968), pp. 257-63.

4 The Turn of the Screw

In the six months following the Czechoslovakian crisis the Soviet Union continued to pursue an essentially defensive strategy based on outward support for the League of Nations and collective security, while covertly seeking to engineer a direct settlement of its differences with Germany and Japan. In this context Stalin's report to the Eighteenth Congress of the CPSU was a finely judged attempt to promote both strands of Soviet foreign policy. Stalin admitted that the Soviet Union was anxious to settle its differences with Germany and Japan:

> We stand for peace and the strengthening of business relations with all countries. That is our position; and we shall adhere to this position so long as these countries maintain like relations with the Soviet Union, and so long as they make no attempt to trespass on the interests of our country.[1]

At the same time the Soviet leader warned Britain and France that only a concerted effort by the powers willing to defend the status quo could halt the escalation of demands emanating from the revisionist nations:

> we are witnessing an open redivision of the world and spheres of influence at the expense of the non-aggressive states, without the least attempt of resistance, and even with a certain amount of connivance, on the part of the latter.
>
> The chief reason is that the majority of the non-aggressive countries, particularly England and France, have rejected the policy of collective security, the policy of collective resistance to

> the aggressors, and have taken up a position of non-intervention, a position of 'neutrality'.[2]

It was perhaps inevitable that Stalin should make this calculated appeal to Britain and France given the cool reception being afforded to Soviet overtures in Berlin and Tokyo. On 15 March 1939, the Soviet Ambassador to London, Ivan Maisky, restated the case for improving Anglo–Soviet relations:

> Our two countries do not always see eye to eye as to the best methods for securing peace, but it is equally true — and the fact is of paramount importance — that at present there is no conflict of interest between the USSR and the British Empire in any part of the world. You will find that in the last resort the fate of peace or war in our time depends on the kind of relations which exist between London and Moscow.[3]

As Maisky spoke, Anglo–Soviet relations were once more being put to the test as German troops occupied Bohemia and Moravia and effectively established a German protectorate over the whole of Czechoslovakia. On 18 March Litvinov denounced the German action as 'arbitrary, violent and aggressive' and refused to recognise the legitimacy of the German protectorate:

> In the opinion of the Soviet Government the actions of the German Government far from eliminating any danger to the general peace, have on the contrary created and enhanced such danger, disturbed political stability in central Europe, enlarged the elements contributing to the state of alarm already created in Europe and dealt a fresh blow to the feeling of security of the nations.[4]

On the same day the British government, fearing that a further German move was imminent, asked the Soviet government to state its position in the event of an act of aggression being committed against Rumania.[5] In reply Litvinov proposed the holding of a conference of representatives from Britain, France, Poland, Rumania, the Soviet Union and Turkey.[6] As *Tass* later noted: 'Such a conference, in the opinion of the Soviet Government, might have provided the greatest possibility for the elucidation of the actual situation and for the definition of the position of all its participants.'[7] It would appear that Litvinov was once again proposing the establishment of a general pact of mutual assistance in Eastern Europe underwritten by guarantees from Britain, France and the Soviet Union. Although in its aim to promote the continuation of the status quo the pact offered certain advantages to the East European states, the scheme was effectively killed by Poland's reluctance to participate in a treaty which might involve the deployment of the Red Army on Polish soil.[8] In recognition of Poland's refusal to participate in a multilateral agreement with the Soviet Union, the British response to Litvinov's initiative limited itself to the proposal that Britain, France, the Soviet Union and Poland sign a declaration agreeing to consult on possible measures to counter any further threat to European security.[9]

Yet if the British government had shown little enthusiasm for the Soviet proposals, the annexation of Czechoslovakia had presented something of a dilemma for the Chamberlain government. The prime minister's immediate reaction was to maintain that Britain could not enter into unlimited commitments in Eastern Europe. On 17 March he declared:

> I feel bound to repeat that, while I am not prepared to engage this country by new unspecified commitments operating under conditions which cannot be foreseen, yet no greater mistake could be made than to suppose that because it believes war to be senseless and a cruel thing, this nation has so lost its fibres that it will not take part to the utmost of its power in resisting such a challenge if it were made.[10]

It would seem, however, that the occupation of Czechoslovakia, which was followed within a week by the German seizure of Memel from Lithuania, destroyed Chamberlain's remaining faith in the value of negotiations with Hitler. On 19 March he noted: 'As soon as I had time to think I saw that it was impossible to deal with Hitler, after he had thrown all his own assurances to the wind.'[11] It was apparent that the Munich agreement was now little more than a flimsy façade and, amid the clamour both within the House of Commons and throughout the nation for resolute action, Chamberlain saw little alternative but to issue a firm and final warning to Germany. The warning took the form of a unilateral British guarantee to Poland issued on 31 March and was followed by the conclusion of an Anglo–Polish defence agreement on 6 April.[12] The British guarantee was explicitly directed against

> any action which threatened Polish independence, and which the Polish Government accordingly considered it vital to resist with their national forces, His Majesty's Government would feel themselves bound at once to lend the Polish Government all the support in their power.[13]

The agreement was seen as a clear warning to Germany that British faith in German assurances was, at long last, exhausted. As German attention turned towards Danzig, it appeared that Britain was prepared to fight rather than permit further German expansion in Europe. In support of this stance similar guarantees were given to

Rumania and Greece,[14] and the British army was seen to be putting itself in a state of readiness with the announcement of measures to double the size of the Territorial Army and the initiation of preparations to introduce conscription.[15] In addition, the choice of a unilateral guarantee rather than the multilateral agreement proposed by the Soviet Union was primarily a concession to Polish demands. While the Polish government was anxious to enlist the support of Britain and France in the maintenance of its independence, it categorically refused to participate in an agreement of mutual assistance with the Soviet Union. Alongside the fear that the Soviet Union would use such an agreement as a pretext to invade Poland lay the threat that Germany would interpret the conclusion of a pact between Poland and the Soviet Union as a hostile act.[16] In order to emphasise this point the German Foreign Minister warned the Polish Ambassador on 21 March 1939, that his government considered that 'a Soviet–Polish understanding would inevitably lead to Bolshevism in Poland'.[17]

The British guarantees to Rumania and Greece represented a significant success for Litvinov. It was hardly surprising that Soviet officials applauded and encouraged an agreement which committed Britain to the maintenance of the status quo in Eastern Europe.[18] The decision, in deference to Polish suspicion to guarantee Poland without extracting a similar commitment from the Soviet Union, radically restructured the balance of power in Eastern Europe. The need for the Soviet Union to bolster Polish resolve to resist the expansion of German influence was now removed. Furthermore, in the event of a military confrontation between Germany and Poland the Soviet Union was now given the option of neutrality while Britain and France carried the burden of maintaining Polish territorial integrity. While, therefore, Litvinov had previously taken the initiative in urging London and Paris to engage in commitments to Eastern Europe, by a strange twist of fate it was now the western powers that sought to enlist Soviet assistance in the containment of German ambitions.

The new-found strength of the Soviet position was indicated by the progressive escalation of the conditions imposed by Litvinov and Molotov for the commitment of the Soviet Union to an East European security pact.[19] On 18 April Litvinov outlined the Soviet position with the unveiling of a scheme based upon the conclusion of an Anglo–French–Soviet pact of mutual assistance. Furthermore, it was proposed that the three nations extend a guarantee against aggression to the countries of Eastern Europe from the Baltic to the Black Sea.[20] It was evident that Litvinov was intent on expanding the Anglo–French commitment to Eastern Europe and, in addition, sought to obtain a pledge of military support in the event of a German assault on the Soviet Union. Such an extensive commitment was rejected by the ish government on 21 April.[21] It was obvious, however, that ɪout the support of the Soviet Union Britain and France could not der direct and effective military assistance to Poland.[22] In an ɜmpt, therefore, to reach a compromise with the Soviet Union, on May the British government agreed, in principle, to the ablishment of a tripartite pact of mutual assistance.[23] Although ferences still existed on the extent of the proposed guarantee to the ɪstern European nations, the proposal was sufficiently well received encourage Neville Chamberlain to despatch William Strang, Head the Central Department of the British Foreign Office, to Moscow ɔr further negotiations. Strang's initial reports from Moscow, owever, indicated that he was under no illusion as to the difficulties to e overcome in engineering an agreement:

> Our need for an agreement is more immediate than theirs.
> This is the strength of their negotiating position and this makes it certain that if we want an agreement with them we shall have to pay their price or something near it.[24]

After four weeks of discussions the gap between the British and Soviet positions remained unbridged. Further complications had been added by Molotov, who raised additional issues with the suggestion that the guarantees to the East European states be expanded to include indirect aggression, such as political subversion, and that military contingency talks be opened to run parallel with the political negotiations. While the British government rejected the inclusion of indirect aggression, which would have effectively given the Soviet Union a free hand to intervene in neighbouring states under the pretext of nullifying political subversion, it was agreed that Anglo–French–Soviet military negotiations be opened in Moscow in August.[25] This decision was indicative of the strength and leverage that the Soviet Union possessed during the course of the negotiations which forced the British into a series of concessions. Strang noted on 20 July: 'it is indeed extraordinary that we should be expected to talk military secrets with the Soviet Government before we are sure that they will be our allies.'[26]

With the opening of formal military negotiations on 12 August a further problem emerged when the Soviet delegation, led by Marshal Voroshilov, demanded an assurance that Poland and Rumania would permit the transit of Soviet forces through their territory to assist Britain and France in the event of German aggression in Western Europe.[27] Although such an agreement was certain to be resisted by both Poland and Rumania, in their bid to clear the path to an agreement the British and French governments agreed to exert pressure for the acceptance of Soviet demands.[28] The outcome of these negotiations was however largely academic for by the third week of August Soviet thoughts were turning almost exclusively to the prospect of a pact of non-aggression with Germany.

The fact that four months of Anglo–French–Soviet negotiations failed to produce an agreement was not altogether surprising given the progressive escalation of the Soviet terms. The value of an agreement with Britain and France was only marginal to Stalin given his conviction that a German assault on Poland or Rumania would result in Hitler becoming enmeshed in an extensive military campaign in Western Europe. As the Soviet Union sought to remain neutral in any such conflict it was likely that only wholesale concessions would have tempted Stalin to ally the Soviet Union with the western powers. On this basis Stalin demanded of Britain and France, as a minimum, a pledge of immediate military support in the event of a German assault on the Soviet Union and recognition of Eastern Europe as an exclusive Soviet sphere of interest. It was this latter demand, which Maisky described to Halifax as 'a sort of Monroe doctrine in Eastern Europe', which effectively precluded any chance of an agreement being reached.[29] It was apparent that neither Britain nor the East European nations were prepared to accept any such understanding. On 4 April 1939, the Polish Foreign Minister, Beck, had candidly warned Halifax that Poland had no intention of entering into an agreement with the Soviet Union:

> in view of the grave tension between Moscow and Berlin it would be dangerous to bring Russia into any discussion.
>
> . . . any pact of mutual assistance between Poland and Russia would bring an immediate hostile reaction from Berlin and would probably accelerate the outbreak of a conflict.
>
> Poland, for her part, was ready to improve her relations with Soviet Russia but would not extend them.[30]

The determination of the Eastern European nations not to afford the Soviet Union an opportunity to expand its influence over their affairs, and the reluctance of the British government to ride roughshod over their wishes, was admitted by Halifax in a communication to Litvinov on 21 April:

> The primary task must be to erect the first essential barrier against aggression in Eastern Europe by making arrangements for the safety of those States most directly menaced. It is only after we have completed this stage that we should be in a position to consider extending any arrangement to other States, like the Soviet Union itself, which are not so immediately threatened. . . .

This does not mean to say that His Majesty's Government do not wish the Soviet Government to be associated with their efforts. On the contrary they are conscious that the support that might be afforded by the Soviet Government to the small East European countries might be of the utmost value in case of war. The difficulty is that the Governments of those countries are reluctant either to engage themselves in a treaty of mutual assistance with the Soviet Union or even publicly to admit that Soviet assistance would be welcome to them.[31]

This preoccupation with Polish sensibilities was a central factor in British strategy throughout the summer. In July after a discussion with the Polish Foreign Minister, Chamberlain concluded:

He was very anxious not to be tied up with Russia, not only because Poles don't like Russians, but because of the effect on German opinion and policy. He thought such an association might lead Hitler to make an attack, which otherwise he hoped it might be possible to avoid. I confess I very much agree with him, for I regard Russia as a very unreliable friend with an enormous irritative power on others.[32]

In this light it was apparent that deep divisions still existed between Britain and the Soviet Union. Certainly, Strang in his reports from Moscow referred repeatedly to the impenetrable barriers of mistrust that clouded the negotiations:

If we do not trust them they equally do not trust us. They are not, fundamentally, a friendly power; but they, like us, are driven to this course by force of necessity. If we are of two minds about the wisdom of what we are doing, so are they.[33]

The Moscow negotiations, therefore, presented the British government with something of a dilemma for, while recognising the advantages that would accrue from a political and military alliance with the Soviet Union, Chamberlain was never able to overcome the suspicion that the Soviet Union was playing at power politics and seeking to manipulate the situation in order to absorb Eastern Europe into its sphere of influence. On 26 March 1939 Chamberlain noted:

I must confess to the most profound distrust of Russia. I have no belief whatever in her ability to maintain an effective offensive even if she wanted to. And I distrust her motives which seem to me to have little connection with our ideas of liberty and to be concerned only with getting every one else by the ears. Moreover she is both hated and suspected by many of the smaller States notably Poland, Rumania and Finland.[34]

Four months later Chamberlain's suspicion of Soviet motives remained unabated:

> I can't believe that she has the same aims and objects as we have, or any sympathy with democracy as such. She is afraid of Germany and Japan and would be delighted to see other people fight them.[35]

This distrust of the Soviet Union explains, in part, why Britain did not pursue the question of an alliance with the Soviet Union with more vigour, and why Chamberlain and Halifax dismissed the suggestion that the British delegation be headed by a senior minister.[36] It would appear, therefore, that Chamberlain still clung to the belief that Britain and France could settle their differences with Germany without recourse to an alliance with the Soviet Union. As late as July 1939 Chamberlain noted: 'if dictators would have a modicum of patience, I can imagine that a way could be found of meeting German claims while safeguarding Poland's independence and economic security.'[37] In this context the British prime minister still saw a direct settlement with Germany as his first priority. Indeed, given the price demanded by the Soviet Union for an alliance which offered Britain an unreliable and untried ally with no guarantee that the outcome would curb German ambitions, the prospect of an Anglo–German agreement must have appeared far more attractive. If Germany, which was seen as the focus of European discontent, could be pacified then an alliance with the Soviet Union would not be necessary.[38] During July and August Chamberlain used his industrial adviser, Horace Wilson, as a link with the German Ambassador to London, Dirksen, in an attempt to engineer an Anglo–German agreement.

If Chamberlain saw the Anglo–Soviet relationship as of only secondary importance, there were certainly other suitors who were anxious to come to an agreement with the Soviet regime. As early as 13 April 1939, the British Ambassador in Moscow, Sir William Seeds, warned the Foreign Secretary:

> I am bound however to point to a possible danger arising either now or in case of war at the stage where Germany had reached the Soviet frontier through Poland, namely an offer by Germany to the Soviet Union of Bessarabia and parts of Poland not to mention perhaps Estonia and Latvia.[39]

The German Foreign Minister, Joachim von Ribbentrop, later stated that the initiative for a Soviet–German *rapprochement* came primarily from the Soviet Union and was first indicated by the tenor of the report delivered by Stalin to the Eighteenth Congress of the CPSU on 10 March 1939.[40] It would, however, be more realistic to conclude that the Soviet Union had continually sought to explore the possibility of a political understanding with Germany in Eastern Europe but that its tentative advances had been continually rebuffed by Germany.[41] It appeared, however, that the events of March had produced a reassessment of this relationship by both parties. Having effectively annexed Czechoslovakia, Hitler now sought to wrest Danzig from Poland. A campaign of intimidation directed against the Polish government culminated, on 21 March, in a meeting between von Ribbentrop and the Polish Ambassador to Berlin, Lipski.[42] Lipski categorically refused to accede to the German demands, and Polish intransigence was further reinforced ten days later by the British guarantee of Polish independence.[43] Faced with an *impasse,* Hitler decided to break Polish resistance by military force, and in April ordered the Commander in Chief of the German Army, Colonel General Walter von Brauchitsch, to commence military preparations for an assault on Poland in September 1939.[44] With this tacit commitment to a war with Poland the attainment of a treaty of non-aggression with the Soviet Union was of central importance to Germany. Such an agreement promised not only to prevent Soviet military assistance being rendered to Poland, therefore eliminating the possibility of Germany being involved in extensive campaigns in both East and West Europe, but would also inhibit the establishment of an Anglo–French–Soviet alliance.[45] If deprived of the assistance of the Red Army, Hitler was satisfied that Britain and France would acquiesce in the German absorption of Poland in a similar fashion to their surrender over the Czechoslovakian issue.[46]

A similar reorientation of Soviet priorities had been undertaken as a result of the British guarantee to Poland. The Soviet Union had been freed of the need to negotiate an alliance with Britain and France in order to deflect German ambitions from its European frontiers. The removal of Litvinov from the position of Commissar for Foreign Affairs on 3 May 1939 was indicative of Stalin's appreciation that the pursuit of collective security was no longer of paramount interest. As early as October 1938 the Counsellor of the German Embassy in Moscow, von Tippelskirch, had concluded that the devaluing of collective security would lead to the removal of Litvinov:

> In the light of our experiences it seems to me probable that Stalin will draw conclusions about personalities from the failure of Soviet policy. In that connection I naturally think in the first place of Litvinov, who has made fruitless efforts in Geneva.[47]

The replacement of Litvinov by Molotov, in essence, served two purposes. First, it was a clear indication to Germany that the Soviet Union was no longer aligned with Britain and France in opposition to the revisionist powers. Secondly, it placed Soviet foreign affairs in the hands of one of Stalin's most senior and trusted lieutenants which was a sign that the Soviet leader saw the months ahead as one of the most crucial periods in the short history of the Soviet state.[48]

In an attempt to strengthen the Soviet position Stalin was prepared, however, to negotiate with both Britain and Germany. In the same week, therefore, that Litvinov proposed to Halifax the conclusion of an Anglo–French–Soviet pact of mutual assistance, the Soviet Ambassador in Berlin, Merekalov, informed the State Secretary of the German Foreign Ministry, Weizsacker, that 'There existed for Russia no reason why she should not live with Germany on a normal footing. And from normal, relations might become better and better.'[49] For once the Germans were prepared to respond to Soviet overtures and, in the following two months, tentative moves were made to explore the possibility of a Soviet–German *rapprochement*. In keeping with the covert nature of Soviet–German relations these informal discussions were conducted under the pretext of economic negotiations between the Counsellor of the Soviet Embassy in Berlin, Astakhov, and the Head of the Economic Section of the East European Department of the German Foreign Ministry, Schnurre. The use of relatively minor officials was indicative of the desire by both nations for secrecy while the grounds for an agreement were explored. On 5 May 1939, Schnurre responded to the initial Soviet probe by assuring Astakhov that Germany would permit the Czechoslovak Skoda Armament Company to fulfil its contracts with the Soviet Union.[50] Taking note of the German concession on this point and the recent cessation of anti-Soviet propaganda in the German press Astakhov, on 17 May, emphasised his belief that relations could be improved and that he saw no reason for continued enmity and distrust in Soviet–German relations. Astakhov concluded: 'It was true that in the Soviet Union there was a distinct feeling of being menaced by Germany. It would undoubtedly be possible to eliminate this feeling of being menaced and the distrust of Moscow.'[51]

Ribbentrop and Weizsacker, who had been watching the Astakhov–Schnurre negotiations with interest, now decided to test Moscow by instructing the German Ambassador to Moscow, Count von der Schulenburg, to propose to Molotov the reopening of German–Soviet economic negotiations.[52] Molotov's response exceeded their expectations in that the Soviet Commissar referred directly to the need to achieve a political understanding as a basis for economic negotiations.[53] With Hitler's announcement to his senior military advisers, on 23 May 1939, that he had elected to take military action against Poland and he was, therefore, exploring the possibility of a Soviet–German understanding the move for an agreement appeared to be gathering momentum.[54] The only remaining area of doubt was the extent of the commitment to be made to the Soviet Union. In a telegram to Schulenburg, dated 26 May, von Ribbentrop indicated that he was already thinking along the lines of a comprehensive agreement envisaging an informal partitioning of Poland:

> Should, contrary to our wishes, hostilities with Poland occur, it is our firm conviction that this would not necessarily lead to a conflict of interests with Soviet Russia. So much we can say even today, that in a solution of the German–Polish problem — whatever the means might be — the greatest possible regard would be paid to Russian interests.[55]

A memorandum by Weizsacker, dated 25 May, however, proposed a more cautious approach based on the continuation of informal economic negotiations and the use of various agencies, such as the Italian Foreign Office, to sound the Soviet Union on the possibility of a political agreement.[56] Weizsacker was probably influenced by reports from Schulenburg that Molotov appeared to be using the German negotiations purely as a lever to extract further concessions from Britain and France.[57] While appreciating the need to disrupt the Soviet Union's relations with Britain and France, Weizsacker, therefore, remained sceptical as to Stalin's sincerity in seeking an agreement with Germany.[58]

It would appear that Hitler largely accepted von Ribbentrop's interpretation of the situation. It was evident that both feared that Anglo–French qualms concerning the extent of the area to be guaranteed in Eastern Europe would not be sufficient to prevent the conclusion of an agreement with the Soviet Union. Chamberlain's announcement on 24 May that an agreement was likely to be established in the near future,[59] and the presentation of the Anglo–French terms to the Soviet Union on 27 May, only served to heighten German apprehension of a Soviet alignment with the western powers.[60] In response, Hitler accepted von Ribbentrop's proposal that immediate steps be taken to explore Molotov's reference, on 20 May, to the possibility of a political understanding. On 30 May, therefore, Gustav Hilger, the economic adviser to the German Embassy, Moscow, was instructed to approach the Soviet Commissar for Trade, Mikoyan, and propose the reopening of economic negotiations.[61] More significantly, however, Weizsacker emphasised to Astakhov that Hitler saw no reason for enmity between Germany and the Soviet Union and was anxious to reopen negotiations for an economic agreement.[62] The direct involvement of Weizsacker in the negotiations and the suggestion that Hitler accepted Molotov's remark that an economic agreement would require certain political bases were clear indications to the

Soviet Union that the Germans were ready to open serious and detailed negotiations. This was confirmed the same day when Weizsacker instructed Schulenburg that the German Foreign Ministry was now prepared to waive its previous reservations as to the desirability of pursuing an understanding with the Soviet Union.[63]

The Soviet response was immediate and encouraging. On 31 May Molotov, in a major address to the Supreme Soviet on the international situation, referred specifically to the likelihood that economic negotiations with Germany would be resumed:

> While conducting negotiations with England and France, we do not by any means think it necessary to renounce business dealings with countries like Germany and Italy.
>
> Judging by certain signs, it is not impossible that the negotiations will be resumed.[64]

In addition, the Commissar for Foreign Affairs roundly criticised the recent Anglo–French proposals which he alluded to as being 'hedged round with so many reservations, including one referring to certain clauses of the League of Nations Covenant, that it may turn out to be a fictitious step forward'.[65] The main stumbling-block appeared to be the Anglo–French reluctance to extend guarantees of independence to the Baltic states. Molotov indicated that the Soviet Union saw such guarantees as a prerequisite for a comprehensive settlement:

> As to guarantees for the countries of central and Eastern Europe, the proposals show no advance if the question is looked at from the point of view of reciprocity. They provide for Soviet assistance to the five countries which the English and French have already promised guarantees, but they say nothing about their help for the three countries on the north west frontier of the USSR which may prove incapable of defending their neutrality in the event of aggression.[66]

With negotiations with the western powers apparently deadlocked Molotov turned once again to Germany. The Soviet Commissar appreciated that an agreement with Germany offered not only an opportunity to defuse the tension in Eastern Europe, but also opened up the possibility of utilising Berlin's links with Tokyo to deflect Japanese ambitions away from the Soviet Far Eastern territories.[67] The potential for the establishment of a Soviet–Japanese *rapprochement* was a powerful bargaining card in von Ribbentrop's hand and, in an attempt to reinforce his position in the last week of May 1939, he urged the Japanese Ambassador, Oshima, to encourage Tokyo to de-escalate border clashes with the Soviets in the Far East. Although Oshima was sceptical as to the possibility of realigning

Japanese policy, von Ribbentrop remained confident that a détente could be engineered which would satisfy the Soviet leadership.[68] In response to a report from the Bulgarian minister querying whether the Soviet Union was now prepared to pursue a pact of non-aggression with Germany,[69] von Ribbentrop informed the Soviet Embassy in Rome that Germany was anxious to conclude such a pact and would also assist in the improvement of Soviet–Japanese relations.[70] Throughout the month of June, however, little progress was made as the Soviet Union continued to give broad indications of its desire for an agreement but persistently evaded the opening of specific discussions. It was evident that the German Foreign Ministry was rapidly losing patience and, on 28 June, von Ribbentrop instructed Schulenburg to press Molotov for clarification of the political preconditions referred to on 29 May.[71] When the Soviet Union again proved evasive Hitler promptly ordered the cessation of all further negotiations.[72]

Soviet reticence in this period can only be accounted for by reference to two factors. First, the belief that, following the British guarantee to Poland, the Soviet position had been significantly strengthened in that it was now Britain, France and Germany that pursued the Soviet Union for an alliance. Secondly, the conviction that Soviet interests were best served by an attempt to extract the maximum concessions from all of the parties concerned. In this context a premature commitment to either side was to be avoided and having established the outlines of the German offer, the Soviet Union once again turned to Britain and France. On 15 June, William Strang arrived in Moscow and was immediately presented with the revised Soviet demands which now raised, for the first time, the question of expanding the guarantee to the Eastern European nations to cover both direct and indirect aggression. Undoubtedly the Soviet government sought to delay negotiations with Germany while the outcome of this new initiative became clear.[73]

For three weeks the lines of communication between Berlin and Moscow remained relatively dormant. The silence was eventually broken on 21 July, when Schulenburg was informed that the Soviet Union wished to reopen negotiations for an economic agreement.[74] On 26 July Schnurre met with Astakhov and Barbarin, the head of the Soviet economic mission. Schnurre once again emphasised that German interests did not conflict with the Soviet Union in either Europe or the Far East and, therefore, he saw no obstacle to the conclusion of a political agreement. For once the Soviet delegates responded positively. While agreeing with Schnurre, in principle, Astakhov alluded to the Soviet Union's suspicion that Germany saw the Baltic states, Finland and Rumania as lying within its sphere of interest. While Astakhov indicated that the Soviet government was prepared to discuss this matter at a senior level, it was apparent that Stalin had at last named his price for the conclusion of an agreement.[75] This sudden move was precipitated by several factors. First, the failure of the negotiations with Britain and France. Although the British had acceded to the Soviet request for the opening of military staff talks, this decision did little to conceal the marked failure to engineer a mutually acceptable political basis for an agreement. Secondly, Stalin appreciated that the German campaign against Poland was moving towards a crisis point. Following reports that Hitler was intent on settling the Polish question in the autumn of 1939, Stalin appreciated that the question of a German alliance would have to be resolved within the coming month.[76] If the Soviet Union continued to evade the German advances there was a distinct possibility that Hitler would seek some form of compromise with Britain and France over the Polish question which would result in Germany establishing itself as a powerful and threatening neighbour on the Soviet Union's western frontiers.[77] In that the strength of the Soviet bargaining position would evaporate with the disappearance of Poland, Stalin had little option but to explore fully the possible benefits that could be derived from a German alliance.

Given Hitler's determination to settle the Polish issue in the last week of August, the Soviet willingness to reopen negotiations was greeted in Berlin with immense relief. The immediate priority was to ensure Soviet neutrality in the event of a German assault on Poland. To this end Weizsacker instructed Schulenburg on 29 July to inform Molotov that Germany acknowledged the extent of Soviet interests in Poland:

> In every development of the Polish question, be it in a peaceful manner as we wish or be it in another manner forced upon us, we would be prepared to safeguard all Soviet interests and to come to an understanding with their government.[78]

In addition, von Ribbentrop personally informed Astakhov, on 2 August, of his belief that it was possible to remodel German–Soviet relations and eliminate the possibility of a future clash of interests in Eastern Europe.[79] This clear indication that Germany was willing to divide Eastern Europe into spheres of influence was accompanied by a further reference to the possibility of engineering an improvement of Soviet–Japanese relations.

Despite these initiatives it was soon apparent, however, that Molotov was still playing for time. On 3 August, the Soviet Commissar for Foreign Affairs suggested that relations could not be improved while Germany remained a central figure in the Anti-Comintern pact. Schulenburg concluded:

> From Molotov's whole attitude it was evident that the Soviet Government was in fact more prepared for improvement in German–Soviet relations but that the old mistrust of Germany persists. My overall impression is that the Soviet Government is at present determined to sign with England and France if they fulfil all Soviet wishes. Negotiations, to be sure, might still last a long time, especially since mistrust of England is also great. I believe that my statements made an impression on Molotov; it will nevertheless take a considerable effort on our part to cause the Soviet Government to swing about.[80]

Whether or not Molotov still held faith in the possibility of an agreement with Britain and France or whether he was once again delaying with the hope of forcing further concessions from both parties is largely a matter for conjecture. It is interesting to note, however, that the attempt to slow the pace of the German–Soviet *rapprochement* coincided with the opening of Anglo–French–Soviet military negotiations in Moscow on 12 August 1939. It was apparent, however, well before the adjournment of the discussions on 16 August 1939, that the Anglo–French delegation did not have the authority to commit their respective governments to an agreement with the Soviet Union, and could not guarantee that Poland and Rumania would permit the passage of Soviet military forces through their territory. If the Soviet government needed any further proof of Anglo–French inability or unwillingness to meet the Soviet terms, the military discussions quickly confirmed the futility of further discussion.[81]

From this point onwards it appeared that the die was cast. Given the assumption that a German assault on Poland was likely in the near future the Soviet Union turned exclusively to the pursuit of an agreement with Germany. The only questions now to be considered were the terms of the agreement and the timing of its conclusion. On 10 August 1939, Schnurre assured Astakhov that German interests in Poland were limited, and suggested that there would be little difficulty in accommodating Soviet expectations.[82] Molotov, however, indicated that he required a clear statement of the German terms before von Ribbentrop could be received in Moscow.[83] The Soviet Commissar demanded, in addition to a pact of non-aggression, a joint guarantee of the Baltic states and German assistance in the improvement of Soviet–Japanese relations.[84] With the planned assault on Poland due to be launched within two weeks, the Soviet price was largely immaterial and Schulenburg was instructed to agree to Molotov's terms on 16 August 1939.[85] Yet once again Molotov appeared to be delaying when, on 19 August, he presented Schulenburg with the Soviet draft of the proposed pact of non-aggression but refused to receive Ribbentrop before 26 August.[86] At this point it seemed that Hitler's patience was finally exhausted and the following day he intervened personally with a message to Stalin agreeing to the terms of the Soviet draft pact in principle, but demanding that von Ribbentrop be received in Moscow by 23 August at the latest.[87] Faced with this ultimatum Stalin finally capitulated and von Ribbentrop arrived in Moscow on 23 August. The terms of the agreement, concluded the same day, largely paralleled those of the Soviet draft treaty, except that the duration of the pact was extended from five to ten years with the option of renewal for a further five years.[88] The agreement, however, departed from the previous format adopted by the Soviet Union in treaties of non-aggression. First, the treaty was to come into force immediately and, therefore, was not subject to the formal process of ratification. Secondly, it did not become inoperative if either party attacked a third country. The inclusion of these points had been demanded by Germany and clearly indicated Hitler's intention to launch an assault on Poland once Soviet neutrality was secured. In addition, a secret protocol was negotiated which outlined German and Soviet spheres of influence in Eastern Europe. In his determination to forge an agreement von Ribbentrop agreed to Finland, Estonia, Latvia and Bessarabia being recognised as lying within the Soviet sphere of interest. As to the question of Poland, the Rivers Narev, San and Vistula were seen as effectively dividing the Soviet and German spheres.[89]

The conclusion of the pact was greeted as a major triumph in Berlin. From July onwards Hitler had been prepared to agree to the Soviet absorption of the Baltic states and areas of Poland if in return he could secure a guarantee of Soviet neutrality in the event of a German assault on Poland. With this goal achieved Hitler was able to concentrate exclusively on the Polish question secure in the knowledge that without the assistance of the Red Army the Anglo–French guarantee to Poland was virtually worthless in military terms. Furthermore, it appeared that the failure of Britain and France to establish an alliance with the Soviet Union had increased the possibility that they would ultimately renege on their pledges to Poland just as they had effectively deserted Czechoslovakia in 1938. By the last week of August, therefore, Hitler was convinced that his preparations were complete for the invasion of Poland. Not even the conclusion of an Anglo–Polish alliance on 25 August 1939, or last-minute Italian apprehensions could deter the German leader from launching his forces against Poland in September 1939.[90]

The logic of an agreement between Germany and the Soviet Union by the autumn of 1939 was almost irresistible. In the twelve months following the *Anschluss* the German threat to the Soviet Union's western frontiers gained in momentum with the absorption of the Sudetenland and the campaign for the reincorporation of Danzig within the German Reich. Following the occupation of Prague in March 1939, Stalin was confronted with the choice of either renewing links with Britain and France in the hope of deterring further German expansion or seeking an understanding with Germany.[91] It was, in effect, the British guarantee to Poland which settled the issue. Given the assumption that a German assault on Poland was likely to result in Germany being drawn into an extensive military campaign in Western Europe, the prospect of an Anglo–French–Soviet alliance was no longer of particular attraction to the Soviet Union. Such an agreement, which threatened to involve the Soviet Union in a military conflict with Germany, could probably have only been engineered after March 1939 by Anglo–French recognition of the minor East European states from the Baltic to the Black Sea as lying within an exclusive Soviet sphere of interest. When it became apparent that Britain and France were neither able nor willing to pay this price, Soviet attention turned almost exclusively towards negotiations with Berlin. In comparison the German offer was far more lucrative. The Soviet Union was offered extensive territorial gains in Eastern Europe which established a *cordon sanitaire* between Germany and the Soviet Union. In addition, if Britain and France fulfilled their treaty commitments to Poland, the centre of hostilities would quickly gravitate to what promised to be a war of attrition in Western Europe. The suggestion that Hitler would be willing to use his links with Tokyo to defuse Soviet–Japanese military tension in the Far East was an added bonus to what was essentially a European settlement.

The strength of the Soviet bargaining position rested primarily on Hitler's desire to secure Soviet neutrality in the event of a German assault on Poland. Stalin was aware, however, that it was not inconceivable that Hitler, in his determination to settle the Polish issue in the autumn of 1939, would launch his invasion irrespective of a prior agreement with the Soviet Union. It was, therefore, the German ultimatum of 20 August 1939 that forced Stalin to finally come down off the fence, and agree to the conclusion of the German–Soviet pact of non-aggression. This decision was, however, something of a gamble for it was based on the assumption that Poland would physically resist a German invasion and also call upon Britain and France to fulfil their pledges of military assistance. While the statements of the Anglo–French military missions in Moscow in August 1939 and the immediate British reaction to the announcement of the German–Soviet agreement suggested that military assistance would be rendered to

Poland, the matter continued to be the subject of intense debate right up until 3 September. It is interesting to note that throughout August the Soviet Union continued to reassure Poland that it would furnish military supplies in the event of a German invasion of Polish territory. As these pledges were not fulfilled it would appear that they represented an attempt to close the final loophole and ensure that Poland resisted the German aggression and called on Britain and France to fulfil their pledges.[92]

On 3 September it appeared that Stalin's judgement had been vindicated and that the Soviet leader had navigated his country through a period fraught with danger. The Soviet Union held the promise of extensive territorial gains in Eastern Europe. Furthermore, the opening of hostilities in Western Europe seemed to imply that the Soviet Union would be able to maintain a position of neutrality while Germany, Britain and France dissipated their military strength. All in all Stalin's prophecy of 19 January 1925 appeared to have been fulfilled:

> if war breaks out we shall not be able to sit with folded arms. We shall have to take action but we shall be the last to do so. And we shall do so in order to throw the decisive weight into the scales, the weight that can turn the scales.[93]

Yet Stalin's prediction depended upon Hitler's acceptance of the logic of winning the war in Western Europe before turning east. It was the German leader's decision to ignore this precondition in launching an assault on the Soviet Union in 1941 that upset Stalin's calculations and almost led to the extinction of the Soviet state.

In reviewing the events that led to the conclusion of the Molotov–Ribbentrop pact there has been a tendency to see Soviet policy as both immoral and Machiavellian. Certainly Churchill sought to chastise the Soviet Union for deserting collective security after the Czechoslovak crisis in 1938 and for actively encouraging the assault upon Poland in September 1939:

> If a government has no moral scruples it often seems to gain great advantages and liberties of action but 'All comes out even at the end of the day and will come out yet more even when all the days are ended.'[94]

Yet it is equally valid to contend that in its efforts to maintain the status quo in Eastern Europe the Soviet Union in the period 1934–39 was a loyal and fervent advocate of collective security. The failure to secure a broad alliance with Britain and France capable of restraining German ambitions must be placed squarely at the feet of the western allies. It was their handling of the major international crises of the

1930s which progressively eroded confidence in the cause of collective security. In a decade of missed opportunities French and British leaders consistently preferred to appease Berlin, Rome and Tokyo rather than attempt to harness Soviet strength to the defence of international stability. Although Soviet interests were largely confined to Eastern Europe and the Far East the establishment of multilateral security agreements in these regions might well have changed the course of history. Instead the western statesmen displayed a greater suspicion of Soviet communism than of the growing fascist menace.

In this context it was hardly surprising that Moscow did not pin its faith on the establishment of a relationship with Britain and France and insisted on keeping open its lines of communication with Berlin. Following the British guarantee to Poland, a Soviet–German agreement was both logical and expedient from the Soviet viewpoint. If Britain and France were slow to appreciate the rationale underpinning Soviet policy, there was every indication that Germany understood the change in the balance of power which resulted from the British guarantee to Poland. In one sense, however, little had changed, for Stalin had clearly established the basic tenet of Soviet foreign policy in January 1934: 'Our orientation in the past and our orientation of the present time is toward the USSR and toward the USSR alone.'[95] If in 1934 the defence of Soviet interests had demanded that the Soviet Union join the League of Nations and seek broad collaboration with the powers promoting the cause of collective security, it was equally logical from the Soviet point of view that the maintenance of those same interests, in August 1939, demanded the conclusion of the Soviet–German pact of non-aggression. As Molotov stated on 31 August 1939, after deriding the efforts of Britain and France to engineer an understanding with the Soviet Union on their own terms:

> the British and French Governments are afraid that the conclusion of a real pact of mutual assistance with the USSR may strengthen our country — the Soviet Union, which it appears does not answer their purpose. One cannot but see that their fears outweigh other considerations.[96]

The Soviet Union, however, had no such fears or scruples, as Molotov candidly admitted:

> Is it really difficult to comprehend that the USSR is pursuing and will continue to pursue its own independent policy based on the interests of the peoples of the USSR and only these interests?[97]

It was this perspective that made the logic of the German–Soviet pact virtually irresistible in the summer of 1939.

Notes

1. Jane Degras (ed.), *Soviet Documents on Foreign Policy*. Vol. 3: *1933–1941* (New York, 1978), Stalin's report to the Eighteenth Congress of the CPSU, 19 March 1939, pp. 315-22.
2. Ibid., p. 318.
3. Quoted in Max Beloff, *The Foreign Policy of Soviet Russia*. Vol. II: *1936–1941* (London, 1949), p. 220.
4. Degras, Note from Litvinov to German Ambassador in Moscow, 18 March 1939, pp. 322-3.
5. *Soviet Peace Efforts on the Eve of World War Two*. Vol. I, Telegram from Soviet Ambassador in Britain to Litvinov, 18 March 1939, pp. 254-5.
6. Ibid., Telegram from Litvinov to Soviet Ambassadors in London and Paris, 18 March 1939, p. 256.
7. Degras, *Tass* statement, 22 March 1939, p. 324.
8. Beloff, pp. 230-1.
9. *Soviet Peace Efforts on the Eve of World War Two*. Vol. I, Telegram from Soviet Ambassador in Britain to Litvinov, 20 March 1939, pp. 267-8.
10. Quoted in K. Feiling, *The Life of Neville Chamberlain* (London, 1946), p. 400.
11. Ibid., p. 401.
12. *Soviet Peace Efforts,* pp. 299, 318.
13. Ibid., p. 299.
14. Ibid., Declaration by the British Government on guarantees to Rumania and Greece, 13 April 1939, pp. 338-9.
15. Feiling, p. 404.
16. Louis Fischer, *Russia's Road from Peace to War* (New York, 1969), pp. 324-5.
17. Quoted in Beloff, p. 232.
18. Fischer, p. 328.
19. For accounts of these negotiations see Beloff, pp. 225-74; Fischer, pp. 322-67; and William Strang, *Home and Abroad* (London, 1956), pp. 156-98.
20. *Soviet Peace Efforts,* Proposal presented by Litvinov to British Ambassador in USSR, 17 April 1939, pp. 346-7.
21. Ibid., Telegram from Soviet Ambassador in Britain to Litvinov, 21 April 1939, p. 350.
22. See Haigh, Morris and Peters, 'European Rearmament Policies and their Effect on the Balance of Military Power from Munich 1938 to the Outbreak of War 1939', Sheffield City Polytechnic, Department of Political Studies Occasional Paper, Molotov–Ribbentrop Pact No. 10, pp. 54-60, 89-91.
23. *Soviet Peace Efforts,* Vol. 2, Draft agreement between Great Britain, France and the USSR handed by British Ambassador in USSR to Molotov, 27 May 1939, pp. 64-6.
24. Quoted in Fischer, p. 348. See also Strang, pp. 173-98.

25. See ibid., pp. 173-98; Beloff, pp. 254-8; and Fischer, pp. 348-51.
26. Quoted ibid., p. 349.
27. For records of the Moscow military negotiations during the first session (12-16 Aug.) see *Soviet Peace Efforts,* Vol. 2, Document nos. 411, 415, 417, 425, 426, 429.
28. See ibid., Document nos. 432, 435, 438, 441.
29. Quoted in Fischer, p. 348.
30. Ibid., p. 324.
31. Ibid., p. 333.
32. Feiling, p. 408.
33. Quoted in Fischer, p. 349.
34. Feiling, p. 403.
35. Ibid., p. 408.
36. For example, Anthony Eden, the only British minister to have met Stalin, offered to accompany the British delegation to Moscow. This offer was rejected along with suggestions that either Halifax or Chamberlain should undertake the mission. See Lewis Broad, *Anthony Eden* (London, 1955), pp. 132-4.
37. Feiling, p. 407.
38. For documents relating to the Anglo–German discussions in the summer of 1939 see *Documents and Materials,* Vol. 2, Document nos. 12-29.
39. Quoted in Fischer, p. 327.
40. Joachim von Ribbentrop, *The Ribbentrop Memoirs* (London, 1954), p. 109.
41. Weinberg, *Germany and the Soviet Union* (Leiden, 1954), pp. 8-11.
42. Ibid., p. 21; Fischer, p. 323.
43. *Soviet Peace Efforts,* Vol. I, Statement by the British Prime Minister on guarantees to Poland, 31 March 1939, p. 299.
44. A. Rossi, *The Russo–German Alliance* (London, 1950), pp. 11-12.
45. Weinberg, *Germany and the Soviet Union,* p. 22.
46. Gerhard L. Weinberg, *The Foreign Policy of Hitler's Germany,* Vol. II, *Starting World War II, 1937–1939* (University of Chicago, 1980), pp. 675-7.
47. *Documents on German Foreign Policy, 1918–1945,* Series D, Vol. IV, pp. 602-5.
48. For accounts of Litvinov's resignation see Henry L. Roberts, *Maxim Litvinov* in Craig and Gilbert, *The Diplomats 1913–1939,* Vol. 2 (New York, 1977), pp. 373-5, and A. Upham-Pope, *Maxim Litvinov* (London, 1943), pp. 440-2.
49. United States, Department of State, *Nazi–Soviet Relations, 1939–1941, Documents from the archives of the German Foreign Office,* ed. Sontag and Beddie (Washington, 1948), p. 2.
50. Ibid., p. 3.
51. Ibid., pp. 4-5.
52. Weinberg, *Germany and the Soviet Union,* p. 26.
53. Rossi, p. 17; Fischer p. 336.
54. Weinberg, *op cit,* p. 27.

55. Ibid., pp. 27-8.
56. Ibid., pp. 28-9.
57. *Nazi–Soviet Relations,* pp. 7-9.
58. Ibid., pp. 5-7.
59. Weinberg, *op cit,* p. 27.
60. *Soviet Peace Efforts,* Vol. 2, Draft Agreement between Great Britain, France and the USSR handed by British Ambassador to Molotov, 27 May 1939, pp. 64-6.
61. Weinberg, *op cit,* p. 31.
62. Ibid., pp. 30-1; Rossi, p. 18.
63. Fischer, p. 340.
64. Degras, Speech by Molotov at the Supreme Soviet, 31 May 1939, pp. 332-40.
65. Ibid., p. 336.
66. Ibid., pp. 336-7.
67. For a discussion of Soviet–Japanese border clashes in this period, see Alvin D. Coox, *Anatomy of a Small War. The Soviet–Japanese struggle for Changkufeng-Khasan, 1938* (Greenwood, 1977).
68. Weinberg, *op cit,* p. 30.
69. Rossi, p. 18.
70. Ibid.
71. *Nazi–Soviet Relations,* pp. 26-7.
72. Ibid., p. 31.
73. For an account of the Strang mission, see Strang, pp. 173-98; Beloff, p. 254; Fischer, p. 348.
74. Weinberg, *op cit,* p. 37.
75. *Nazi–Soviet Relations,* pp. 32-6.
76. For example the Soviet spy, Richard Sorge, is alleged to have informed Moscow of Hitler's decision to attack Poland on 1 September 1939 as early as the spring of that year. Fischer, p. 335.
77. For German reports on the negotiations with Britain in July and August 1939, see *Documents and Materials,* Vol. 2, Document nos. 12-29.
78. *Nazi–Soviet Relations,* p. 39.
79. Ibid., pp. 37-9.
80. Ibid., p. 39.
81. For an account of the military negotiations see *Soviet Peace Efforts,* Vol. II, Document nos. 412, 413, 415, 417, 425, 426, 429, 435.
82. *Nazi–Soviet Relations,* pp. 44-6.
83. Ibid., pp. 48-9.
84. Ibid., pp. 52-7.
85. Beloff, p. 266; Fischer, p. 361.
86. Beloff, p. 266.
87. Weinberg, *op cit,* p. 45.
88. For comparison see Beloff, pp. 269-70; Degras, Soviet draft for a non-aggression pact with Germany, 19 August 1939, p. 358.
89. Weinberg, *op cit,* p. 48.
90. See Weinberg, *The Foreign Policy of Hitler's Germany,* Vol. 2, pp. 628-55. Also R. H. Haigh, D. S. Morris and A. R. Peters, 'From

Non-Aggression to Barbarossa: German–Soviet relations September 1939–June 1941', Sheffield City Polytechnic, Department of Political Studies Occasional Paper, Molotov–Ribbentrop Pact No. 13; 'The Rise and Rise of the Third Reich. German Foreign Policy 1933–1939', Sheffield City Polytechnic, Department of Political Studies Occasional Paper, Molotov–Ribbentrop Pact No. 14.

91. Isaac Deutscher, *Stalin, A Political Biography* (London, 1966), pp. 422-3.
92. Weinberg, *op cit,* p. 627.
93. Degras, Vol. 2, Stalin's report to the Central Committee of the Russian Communist Party, 19 January 1925, pp. 1-2.
94. Winston S. Churchill, *The Second World War.* Vol. 1: *The Gathering Storm* (London, 1948), p. 307.
95. Degras, Report by Stalin to the Seventeenth Congress of the CPSU, 26 January 1934, pp. 65-72.
96. Ibid., Speech by Molotov to the Fourth Special Session of the Supreme Soviet, 31 August 1939, pp. 363-71.
97. Ibid., p. 371.

5 Conclusion

In examining Soviet relations with the western powers it is tempting to divide the interwar era into three distinct periods. The most striking era was undoubtedly the first six years of the regime when the Soviet state set a defiant face to the world with Trotsky's dramatic denunciation of the treaties entered into by the Tsarist state and his scornful rejection of the informal ground-rules of international diplomacy. It was a strategy based upon the conviction that the sparks of November 1917 were but a preliminary to the ignition of a global revolution of the oppressed against their capitalist overlords. Indeed, Lenin's analysis of 'imperialism' and Trotsky's advocation of 'permanent revolution' had paved the way for an uprising in nations where industrialisation was still in its infancy and, therefore, there was every expectation that the events of November 1917 would unleash a tidal wave of revolutionary war.[1]

This initial period of revolutionary fervour was, however, relatively short-lived. Any hopes that might have existed of similar uprisings in the advanced West European states were effectively doused in 1923 when the last embers of the revolt staged by the German Communist Party were extinguished. There were indications, though, that the Bolsheviks had been forced to readjust their approach to foreign affairs well before the events of 1923. Given the absence of extensive international support Lenin conceded, in 1919, that the initial goal of the Soviet state must be survival while the revolutionary forces consolidated their position and the conditions for global revolution matured. In such a climate Lenin had little option but to seek a détente with the western powers with the object of improving relations and delaying a confrontation until it could be conducted on terms favourable to the forces of revolutionary change. While, therefore, maintaining that a collision between the capitalist and socialist worlds was inevitable, the need for a period of peaceful coexistence became a prominent feature in Soviet strategy.[2] The symbol of this shift in emphasis was the progressive upgrading of the role and status of the Narkomindel and the gradual erosion of the significance attached to the activity of the Comintern. The conclusion of the Treaty of Rapallo in 1922 indicated quite clearly that the instinct for self-preservation dictated that the Soviet state seek an understanding with at least one of the western powers and access to the economic expertise held by the advanced industrial nations. Within six years, therefore, the Soviets had moved from a position of unremitting hostility to the capitalist world to a situation where the opening of diplomatic links and participation in international conferences and agreements was a central factor in Soviet strategy.

The consolidation of the concept of peaceful coexistence is generally associated with Stalin. While Lenin refused to admit that détente with the capitalist world could be anything but transitory and fleeting, it was Stalin who, as early as 1925, spoke of the need to collaborate with the western powers for a period of over two decades while the conditions for revolution ripened.[3] Although the Soviet leader maintained that a collision of interests was inevitable in the long term, he effectively abandoned the last vestiges of Trotsky's commitment to revolutionary war and propelled the Soviet state into the arena of international politics. With the opening of diplomatic ties with most of the major European powers and membership of the League of Nations, the Soviet state apparently sought the mantle of international respectability, abandoning the ideological chasm which divided it from the western powers. Such was the change in the style and tenor of Soviet diplomacy that, while Lenin had denounced the western powers as 'imperialist' and predicted a series of 'frightful collisions', Stalin could declare: 'We stand for peace and the strengthening of business relations with all countries.'[4]

In attempting to evaluate Soviet foreign policy in this period it is difficult to discount the suspicion that much of the rhetoric directed from Moscow was for domestic rather than foreign consumption. Certainly the twists and turns in Soviet strategy that can be traced through the interwar period correspond closely with the course of internal power-struggles within the Soviet state. The exhortations in the early years to promote a revolutionary war and the warnings of the determination of the western powers to crush the nascent Soviet state can be seen as a powerful weapon used to justify draconian economic and military measures and the gravitation of power to an effective dictatorship. It was surely no coincidence that when, in 1928, Stalin returned to the theme of 'capitalist encirclement' and the imminence of a clash of interests, his words were a prelude to the opening of a further round of massive economic and social upheaval in Soviet society. In addition, the resurrection of the prospect of revolutionary war was used by the Soviet leader as ammunition in his campaign to purge elements of the Communist Party.[5]

It is tempting, therefore, to see the utilisation of Marxist–Leninist terminology as merely a veneer manipulated by a political faction to justify the creation and maintenance of a dictatorship. Indeed, the rapidity with which Stalin was able to abandon his prediction of an escalation of conflict in favour of the promotion of a United Front suggested that ideological fervour was continually tempered by pragmatism. The search for alliances with the western powers, membership of the League of Nations and callous manipulation of the Comintern indicated that Stalin gave priority to the maintenance of the Soviet state above that of promoting international revolution. While, perhaps, this could be justified, in that it was seen as important to secure the Soviet state while the capitalist system reached the final stage of collapse, it was clear that a certain continuity could be identified if the tactics pursued by the Soviet state were compared with those of its Tsarist predecessors. In that Stalin sought to anchor Soviet interests in the traditional manner of dividing opponents and engineering a balance of power capable of deterring aggression, the series of treaties conducted with the western powers could be seen as a simple reassertion of the concert of Europe with Stalin assuming the mantle of the Russian Tsars. In attempting to account for the collapse of collective security in 1939 it would seem, therefore, that the Soviet Union, France and Britain ignored the logic of 'balancing' power in Europe and, therefore, assisted the unleashing of aggression:

> Each of Germany's future enemies was torn between the illusion that war could be avoided and the dim awareness of its inevitability. Each was terrified by the danger of isolation and each made some moves towards building up a protective system of alliances. Each shirked definite military commitments, fearing that such commitments might bring war nearer to its own frontiers. In every member of the future Grand Alliance the hope was alive that the impetus of resurrected German militarism might be diverted in some direction indifferent to his national interest.
>
> Each of the future allies sold space for time and let down allies and friends, until no space was left to be sold and time to be bought.[6]

Such an analysis, however, threatens to ignore the impact of ideology on the conduct of Soviet foreign policy. While undoubtedly economic and military weakness forced Lenin and Stalin towards a tacit acceptance of the need to open a dialogue with the western powers, the opening of diplomatic relations could not disguise the suspicion and hostility which divided the Soviet Union from the bulk of the international community. The adherence of the Soviet state to the basic tenets of Marxist–Leninist ideology was a central factor in justifying the pre-eminence of the Communist Party machine in Soviet society. Although Stalin may have wished to temper its impact on relations with the western powers he could not deny that his position in Soviet society was underpinned by an ideology that sought the destruction of the capitalist world.[7]

In this light although Stalin attempted to manoeuvre the Soviet Union into the mainstream of international diplomacy, it was hardly surprising that the Soviet state was continually regarded by the western powers with thinly-veiled suspicion and distrust. In an atmosphere where Britain and France saw events in Spain and the promotion of the United Front as further evidence of the march of international communism the League of Nations was never likely to achieve the degree of cohesion and trust necessary to promote collective security. Indeed, the proceedings at Geneva were already hampered by the determination of the western powers to place national interest, in its narrowest form, before observance of the Covenant. If the Manchurian, Abyssinian and Rhineland crises had led to the suspicion that Britain and France had no intention of allowing an international agency to determine the course of European affairs, the final collapse of the League was confirmed in 1938 and 1939 when Geneva was not invited even to discuss the dismemberment of Czechoslovakia or the German campaign against Poland. It was apparent that while there was general agreement that the League could act as a moral force and an instrument to determine if an act of aggression had been committed, the decision to undertake economic or military sanctions lay solely with individual states.

It was perhaps ironic that the last act of the League was the decision taken by the Council, in December 1939, to expel the Soviet Union following its assault on Finland in November. Given that the Soviet Union had been continually one of the most strident advocates of collective security, with Litvinov continuing to attend the sessions at Geneva even when the western powers had opted to exclude the League from the Czechoslovakian issue, it was cruel twist of fate that the League should condemn the Soviet Union for abandoning collective security and adopting the tactics of its adversaries. In response to the Council's announcement *Tass,* on 16 December, described the decision as 'incomprehensible' and placed the responsibility for 'deserting the League of Nations' squarely on the shoulders of Geneva's 'Anglo–French managers'.[8] There is a certain element of truth in this accusation as F. P. Walters noted:

> In their anxiety to propitiate the Axis powers, the French and British had forced the Russian government against its will, into a position of isolation. It had not, before Munich, wished to be free from the commitments of collective security. But having had that freedom thrust upon it, it decided in the end to reject the approaches of the democracies and accept those of Hitler. A disastrous decision for itself and the world: but one for which the Russians do not bear all the responsibility.[9]

Yet it has to be conceded that the Soviet Union had also contributed to the climate of insecurity. Alongside its boisterous commitment to collective security lay the suspicion that its interests were restricted to Eastern Europe and the Far East. In addition, Britain and France were aware that the possibility of a bilateral agreement with Germany was never excluded from Soviet calculations. Stalin, therefore, amplified the fears of the western powers, encouraged the ambitions of the revisionist nations and assisted the degeneration of European diplomacy into what Eleanor Rathbone called:

> a clever plan of selling your friends in order to buy off your enemies — which has the danger that a time comes when you have no friends left, and then you find you need them, and then it is too late to buy them back.[10]

In essence the establishment of a balance of power capable of deterring German ambitions in the 1930s required the recognition by Britain, France and the Soviet Union of the threat to their common interests mounted by Hitler and a willingness to submerge their differences to counter the German menace. However rational such a course of action may have appeared it was effectively forestalled by selfish miscalculations as to the nature of National Socialist ambitions which were further fuelled by a cloud of mistrust as to the ultimate compatibility of Soviet and Anglo–French interests. Despite Stalin's attempts to bridge the ideological chasm, he failed to remove the deep-seated prejudices that clouded relations and eventually lured the Soviet Union, Britain and France along the treacherous path of accommodation with Hitler's Germany rather than the logic of containment.

Notes

1. For an analysis of the contributions made by Lenin and Trotsky to the evolution of Marxism, see G. M. Sabine, *A History of Political Theory* (London, 1963), Chs 13-15. In addition, R. Carew Hunt, *The Theory and Practice of Communism. An Introduction* (New York, 1957); Elliot Goodman, *The Soviet Design for a World State* (New York, 1960); Alfred Meyer, *Leninism* (Cambridge, 1957); and Robert Tucker (ed.), *The Lenin Anthology* (New York, 1975).
2. For a discussion of Lenin's approach to foreign affairs in this period, see Frederic S. Burin, 'The Communist Doctrine of the Inevitability of War', *American Political Science Review,* June 1963.
3. Isaac Deutscher, *Stalin. A Political Biography* (Harmondsworth, 1966), pp. 388-9.
4. J. Stalin, *Problems of Leninism* (Moscow, 1953), p. 758.
5. Goodman, pp. 129-63.
6. Deutscher, p. 409.
7. For an analysis of the role of ideology in Soviet foreign policy, see Joseph L. Nogee and Robert H. Donaldson, *Soviet Foreign Policy since World War II* (New York, 1981), Ch 2.
8. Jane Degras (ed.), *Soviet Documents on Foreign Policy,* Vol. 3, *Tass* statement, 16 December 1939.
9. F. P. Walters, *A History of the League of Nations* (London, 1969), p. 800.
10. Quoted from N. Thompson, *The Anti-Appeasers* (Oxford, 1971), p. 27.

Bibliography

Official Papers

Documents on British Foreign Policy 1919–39, 2nd series, Vols 1-18 (London, 1946–80); 3rd series, Vol. 1 (London, 1948).

Documents on German Foreign Policy 1918–48, Series C, Vols 1-6, and Series D, Vols 1-4 (London, 1949–83).

Foreign Relations of the United States, 1937, Vol. 3, and 1938, Vol. 1 (Washington, D.C., 1954–55). *The Soviet Union 1933–39* (Washington, D.C., 1952).

Soviet Documents on Foreign Policy, ed. J. Degras, Vol. 1: *1917–24,* Vol. 2: *1925–32,* Vol. 3: *1933–41* (1978) published by OUP for the RIIA.

Nazi–Soviet Relations 1939–41, Documents from the Archives of the German Foreign Ministry, ed. Sontag and Beddie (Washington, D.C., 1948).

Soviet Peace Efforts on the Eve of World War Two. Documents and Records, Vols 1–2 (Moscow, 1973).

Documents and Material in Relation to the Eve of the Second World War, Vol. 1 (Moscow, 1948).

Documents on International Affairs, ed. M. Curtis, Vol. 1: 1938 (London, 1942).

United Kingdom Parliamentary Debates, House of Commons, 5th series, Vol. 169-332.

Books

Abramovitch, Raphael, *The Soviet Revolution 1917–37* (London, 1962).

Beloff, Max, *The Foreign Policy of Soviet Russia,* Vol. 1, *1929–36* (London, 1947) and Vol. 2, *1936–41* (London, 1949) published by OUP for the RIIA.

Byrnes, J.F., *Speaking Frankly* (London, 1947).
Carr, E.H., *German–Soviet Relations between Two World Wars 1919–39* (Baltimore, 1951).
Churchill, W.S., *The Second World War,* Vol. 1: *The Gathering Storm* (London, 1948).
Coox, Alvin D., *Anatomy of a Small War. The Soviet–Japanese struggle for Changkufeng-Khasan, 1938* (Greenwood, 1977).
Craig, G.A. and Gilbert, F. (eds), *The Diplomats 1919–1939,* Vol. 1: *The Twenties* (New York, 1972); Vol. 2: *The Thirties* (New York, 1977). Originally published by Princeton University Press.
Davies, Joseph E., *Mission to Moscow* (London, 1944).
Deutscher, Isaac, *Stalin, A Political Biography* (Harmondsworth, 1977).
Dirksen, Herbert von, *Moscow, Tokyo, London* (London, 1951).
Dreifort, John E., *Yvon Delbos at the Quai D'Orsay* (Kansas, 1973).
Dyck, Harvey L., *Weimar Germany and Soviet Russia 1926–1933* (London, 1966).
Eden, Anthony, *The Eden Memoirs,* Vol. I: *Facing the Dictators* (London, 1962).
Edwards, J., *The British Government and the Spanish Civil War* (London, 1979).
Emmerson, J.T., *The Rhineland Crisis* (London, 1977).
Epstein, Fritz T., *Germany and the East* (Bloomington, Ind., 1973).
Erickson, J., *The Soviet High Command 1918–41* (London, 1962).
Eudin, X.J. and Fisher, H. (eds), *Soviet Russia and the West 1920–27* (Stanford, 1967).
——— and Slusser, R.M., *Soviet Foreign Policy 1928–34* (New York, 1966).
Feiling, K., *The Life of Neville Chamberlain* (Macmillan, London, 1946).
Fischer, Louis, *Men and Politics* (New York, 1941).
——— *The Soviets in World Affairs,* Vols 1 and 2 (Princeton, N.J., 1951).
——— *Russia's Road from Peace to War* (New York, 1969).
Freund, G., *Unholy Alliance. Russo–German Relations from the Treaty of Brest-Litovsk to the Treaty of Berlin* (London, 1957).
Furnia, Arthur H., *The Diplomacy of Appeasement, Anglo–French relations and the prelude to World War II 1931–8* (Washington, D.C., 1960).
Gibbs, N.H., *Grand Strategy,* Vol. 1: *Rearmament Policy* (HMSO, London, 1976).
Goodman, Elliot, *The Soviet Design for a World State* (New York, 1960).
Grey, Ian, *The First Fifty Years, Soviet Russia 1917–67* (London, 1967).
Haynes, Paul, *The Twentieth Century* (London, 1978).
Hilger, G. and Meyer, A., *The Incompatible Allies: A Memoir History of German–Soviet Relations* (New York, 1953).
Hunt, R. Carew, *The Theory and Practice of Communism. An Introduction* (New York, 1957).
Kennan, George F., *Soviet Foreign Policy 1917–41* (Princeton, N.J., 1960).
——— *Russia and the West under Lenin and Stalin* (Boston, 1961).
Koblyakov, I.K., *USSR: For Peace against Aggression, 1933–1941* (Moscow, 1976).
Kochan, Lionel, *Russia and the Weimar Republic* (Cambridge, 1954).

Korbel, Josef, *Poland between East and West* (Princeton, N.J., 1963).
Lloyd-George, David, *Memoirs of the Peace Conference,* Vols 1 and 2 (London, 1938).
Mau, Hermann and Krausnick, Helmut, *German History 1933–45* (New York, 1963).
Meyer, Alfred, *Leninism* (Cambridge, 1957).
Micaud, Charles A., *The French Right and Nazi Germany 1933–39. A Study of Public Opinion* (New York, 1972).
Mosley, Philip (ed.), *The Soviet Union 1922–62, A Foreign Affairs Reader* (New York, 1963).
Nere, J., *The Foreign Policy of France from 1914–1945* (London, 1975).
Nogee, Joseph and Donaldson, Robert, *Soviet Foreign Policy since World War II* (New York, 1981).
Petrie, Sir Charles, *The Life and Letters of the Rt Hon. Sir Austen Chamberlain,* Vol. II (London, 1940).
Preston, Adrian, *General Staffs and Diplomacy before the Second World War* (London, 1978).
Ribbentrop, Joachim von, *The Ribbentrop Memoirs* (London, 1954).
Ripka, H., *Munich: Before and After* (London, 1939).
Robertson, E.M., *Hitler's Pre-War Policy and Military Plans 1933–39* (London, 1963).
Roskill, Stephen, *Hankey, Man of Secrets.* Vol. III: *1931–63* (London, 1974).
Rosser, Richard F., *An Introduction to Soviet Foreign Policy* (New Jersey, 1969).
Rossi, A., *The Russo–German Alliance* (London, 1950).
Sabine, G.M., *A History of Political Theory* (London, 1963).
Schuman, F.L., *Soviet Politics* (London, 1948).
—— *Europe on the Eve* (London, 1942).
Simon, Sir J., *Retrospect* (London, 1952).
Stalin, Joseph, *Problems of Leninism* (Moscow, 1953).
Strang, William, *Home and Abroad* (London, 1956).
Templewood, Viscount, *Nine Troubled Years* (London, 1984).
Thompson, N., *The Anti-Appeasers* (Oxford, 1971).
Thorne, Christopher, *The Limits of Foreign Policy: The West, the League and the Far Eastern Crisis of 1931–33* (London, 1972).
Tucker, Robert (ed.), *The Lenin Anthology* (New York, 1975).
Upham-Pope, Arthur, *Maxim Litvinov* (London, 1943).
Ulam, Adam, *Expansion and Coexistence, the History of Soviet Foreign Policy 1917–67* (London, 1968).
Walters, F.P., *A History of the League of Nations* (London, 1969) published by OUP for the RIIA.
Watt, D.C., *Too Serious a Business, European Armed Forces and the Approach of the Second World War* (London, 1975).
Weinberg, Gerhard L., *The Foreign Policy of Hitler's Germany,* Vol I: *Diplomatic Revolution in Europe 1933–36* (London, 1970); Vol. II: *Starting World War II 1937–39* (Chicago, 1980).
Wheeler-Bennett, J., *Brest-Litovsk, The Forgotten Peace* (London, 1963).
Wolfers, Arnold, *Britain and France between Two Wars* (Harcourt, Brace and Jovanovich, New York, 1966).

Articles

Burin, S., 'The Communist Doctrine of the Inevitability of War', *American Political Science Review,* June 1963.
Carsten, F.L., 'The Reichswehr and the Red Army', *Survey,* October 1962.
Fraenkel, Ernst, 'German–Russian Relations since 1918', *Review of Politics,* January 1940.
Hoffding, W., 'German Trade with the Soviet Union', *Slavonic Review,* Vol. XIV, 1936–37.
Stein, G.H., 'Russo–German Collaboration: The Last Phase, 1933', *Political Science Quarterly,* Vol. LXXVII, March 1962.
Watt, D.C., 'Soviet Military Aid to the Spanish Revolution 1936–38', *Slavonic and East European Review,* June 1960.

Index